Thirteen Steps
to Teacher
Empowerment

Thirteen Steps
to Teacher
Empowerment

Taking a More Active Role in Your School Community

Steven Zemelman

Harry Ross

Foreword by Stephanie Harvey

Heinemann
Portsmouth, NH

Heinemann
361 Hanover Street
Portsmouth, NH 03801–3912
www.heinemann.com

Offices and agents throughout the world

Library of Congress Cataloging-in-Publication Data
Zemelman, Steven.
  Thirteen steps to teacher empowerment : taking a more active role in your school community / Steven Zemelman and Harry Ross.
    p. cm.
  ISBN-13: 978-0-325-01281-0
  ISBN-10: 0-325-01281-4
  1. Teachers—Professional relationships. 2. Educational leadership. I. Ross, Harry. II. Title.
  LB1775.Z46 2009
  371.1—dc22   2009012572

EDITOR: *Lisa Luedeke*
PRODUCTION: *Sonja S. Chapman*
TYPESETTER: *Newgen Imaging*
COVER DESIGN: *Lisa A. Fowler*
AUTHOR PHOTOGRAPH: *Bob Tanner*
MANUFACTURING: *Steve Bernier*

Printed in the United States of America on acid-free paper
13 12 11 10 09 PAH 1 2 3 4 5

Contents

Reach Outside

Foreword

As I sat down and began to read this book, the voice in my head first whispered, then spoke a little louder and finally screamed—Where have you been all my life? *Thirteen Steps to Teacher Empowerment* goes a long way to answer one of education's oldest conundrums. How do we empower teachers to be the very best they can be and free them to create a world where kids can think and learn unfettered? The book begins with narratives of two early career teachers, Jill and Sybil, both of whom want nothing more than to be exceptional educators. Jill's first year is marred with frustration and eventual failure as she struggles in isolation and then sadly drops out of the profession. Sybil meets some rough bumps in the road as well, but reaches out to colleagues both in the school and in the greater education community to connect with mentors and teacher support groups. She goes on to have a productive first year and a wildly successful teaching career. I can't count how many Jills and Sybils I've encountered in my nearly forty years in education. In a profession where 50 percent of new teachers leave in the first five years of teaching, we are desperate for more Sybils! Research tells us again and again that it is the debilitating isolation that nudges so many teachers out of the profession. This book serves as a guide to support teachers to work together in learning communities where teachers plan collaboratively, trust in each other and put kids first.

In this book, Steve Zemelman and Harry Ross invite us to consider five principles that empower teachers to develop into the kind of educators they were meant to be and that allow schools to become places where adults collaborate and make a real difference in the lives of kids. They suggest we start with ourselves by focusing on our own learning, taking a reflective stance and staying positive even when the chips are down. They encourage us to understand the kids more deeply by listening to them carefully, shadowing them, and doing teacher research. They remind us to avoid isolation which threatens to dead end us like it did Jill, and instead, reach out and connect with other teachers. They share that when we get involved in more intentional ways, we come to care about our situation and we even take action, which gives us a better sense of control over our work. And finally, they nudge us to muster outside resources such as community partnerships, professional organizations, and grant writing opportunities to improve schools and to participate in the larger outside-of-school arena.

Jam-packed with practical ideas tucked in between stories of educators you will swear you know personally, *Thirteen Steps* offers countless ideas for turning schools into joyful places that teachers and kids don't want to leave at the end of the day. Steve and Harry recognize that relationships are the key to productive organizations, successful schools and happy teachers. So they fill the book with practical strategies for building trusting relationships with kids, other educators, and community members. They stress that leadership and leader are not the same thing. Rather than viewing leadership as embodied by someone with a powerful personality and organizational authority, their notion of leadership is about the thoughtful and strategic behaviors we can engage in to improve schools, student learning, and teacher satisfaction. With a commitment to this idea of leadership, we can all work more intentionally and effectively to make schools better places for kids and for ourselves.

One thing I love about this book is its simplicity. It is amazingly user friendly. Whether the authors intended it or not, you can jump into this book wherever you see the greatest need. The contents are laid out in such a way that if you are particularly interested in suggestions for connecting with fellow teachers, just head to that section, or if you are doing a project that requires outside resources, go straight to the Reach Outside section. That being said, you don't get off the hook that easily; you must promise to read every word of this book. I didn't come across a sentence that was not worth pondering for a moment or two or a concept that wasn't worthy of some deep thought. This book rocks! So settle down in a comfortable spot with a pen in hand so you can jot in the margins, mark important spots with sticky notes, and fill up the book with your own thoughts.

I have divided my education career equally between classroom teacher and staff developer. From both perspectives, I can't overemphasize the importance of this book. We are draining the life blood out of our schools each time a young Jill decides to leave us. We can't afford to lose the hearts and minds of dedicated people. We can't afford to have kids languishing in dreary schools where people don't trust one another and, worse, don't trust the kids. We need this book and we need it now. It is a road map to a vibrant, thriving, long-lasting teaching life.

—Stephanie Harvey
May 2009

Preface

What is teacher empowerment, and why does it matter for you as an educator? We achieve it when

- we're teaching what we enjoy and know is important, to kids we respect— and we can see they are learning;

- we're treated like professionals, feel like professionals, and have the tools to succeed;

- we have strategies for carving out time for reflection and healthy exercise;

- we collaborate with our colleagues to make our teaching more fruitful;

- we feel in control of our professional lives and encourage others to be successful—in other words, we are exercising informal leadership; and, perhaps most important of all,

- we love to go to work.

This book is for every teacher who wants to make his or her work life more satisfying and more richly connected to the surrounding world, instead of existing defensively behind a closed classroom door. All too often, outstanding progressive teachers become lone rangers, loved by their students but professionally alone in their school. That's simply not as much fun, and it doesn't have to be that way. Of course, if you work in a highly collaborative atmosphere where everyone pitches in together, that's great, and we think the skills explored in this book will help make your work still more efficient and rewarding. But if you are feeling isolated and burning out, we know you'll be happy you picked this volume up.

Both of us have spent many hours in schools teaching kids, listening to teachers, and learning from their well-earned expertise at deepening their teacher power. This book is filled with their stories. However, we have worked in some schools that, while they were not bad places, left teachers hidden behind their doors, working mostly independently. Too many students beyond their own classrooms were anonymous to them. Of course, some teachers collaborated with their friends, but the hallways seemed cold. It wasn't much fun to work there.

We've also worked at schools where teachers shadow students to learn more about how they learn, observe each other teaching and discuss together their successes and challenges, sit on committees that succeed in making valuable improvements to the school, and study students' work together to compare teaching strategies and results and develop new and exciting teaching projects. With teachers collaborating like this, these schools tend to take on a warmth that sometimes belies a rundown building or struggling neighborhood. Working at schools like this can be very exciting.

We experienced this ten years ago at Best Practice High School, a small school in Chicago started by Steve and some colleagues, where you could always feel teachers' and kids' engagement. Since then, we've learned much more about the kinds of wider involvement that can enrich our teaching lives, especially through the work of the Chicago Schools Alliance, a diverse network of schools that have collaborated to strengthen student learning and achieve more sustainability. We'd seen that innovative schools, even the really successful ones, had a hard time surviving, compared with more traditional places. And then we studied Andy Hargreaves' and Dean Fink's *Sustainable Leadership* (2006), which helped us realize teachers' crucial role in developing the whole school as well as their own classrooms. A school that depends solely on the strength of a single, charismatic principal is all too likely to fall on hard times when that person leaves, which, of course, is bound to happen sooner or later. Schools where teachers work together and share leadership have more success and more ways to make the flavor last.

There's also much to learn from the world of community organizing. Our partner in facilitating the Chicago Schools Alliance, Kim Zalent, is highly experienced in that work and has introduced us to skills that most of us teachers rarely think about. Sure, a few faculty members develop as skillful negotiators and step up to become department heads or administrators or leaders of professional organizations. But we can all hone such abilities intentionally, to work more effectively with other adults, whether we're holding any sort of official position or not. Take that person down the hall who looks with disdain on the classroom practices that you love—what's the most effective way to relate to her? Silence at the lunch table? Loud arguments in meetings? Or perhaps a half hour over coffee, one-on-one, where you find out what she really cares about and let her learn about your professional passions as well.

So in this book, we try to dispel myths about leadership: it's not just some formal administrative position exercised from above. It starts with expanding our professional roles in small everyday actions that make our jobs more fulfilling and less difficult. And then we can take on larger school-improvement tasks as we become ready to tackle them. We first encourage you to start with yourself and follow your passions so that teaching can be as fulfilling as possible. In Chapter 1, we offer essential strategies to remain positive and keep growing as a teacher by documenting and reflecting on your teaching, doing some professional reading, exploring new ideas, and taking good care of your health and your own well-being—even if you thought you didn't have the time.

Next comes understanding your kids more deeply, using approaches such as shadowing students throughout a school day (in Chapter 2) and doing some inquiry—with colleagues if possible—to gain more insight into your classroom and your students (Chapter 3).

Then we suggest ways of building stronger professional connections and trust with your colleagues. These include observing other classrooms and inviting fellow teachers into your own (in Chapter 4), as well as understanding more about not only the people you already like but also those with whom you might think you have little in common (in Chapter 5). Such connections and the building of trust are essential not only for your own strength and satisfaction as a teacher but also for the effectiveness of the whole school.

Building on this base, in Chapters 6 and 7 we explore several of the many actions you can take at your school to improve your teaching and the school at the same time—how to create more time for reflection and how to share ideas and broach serious issues in a constructive way that is likely to get positive results. We'll help you learn how to make committee work more productive (in Chapter 8), launch successful campaigns to change instructional practices and school policy (Chapter 9), and develop an effective working relationship with the principal (Chapter 10).

More broadly, we can help you reach beyond the school, working with parents (Chapter 11), getting grants to expand your teaching (Chapter 12), and creating partnerships with universities and nonprofits to give yourself and your students much more access to real-world resources (Chapter 13).

In the conclusion, we describe what a school needs as a whole to develop a true shared vision, a community of trust, a structure for working together, and sustainable whole-school change. While your school may not be there yet, you and every individual teacher can benefit from helping to make this happen.

We don't expect anyone to tackle all this at once. We're mere mortals. But you can consider where you are in your own career, dig into the appropriate chapter of this book, and find among our range of strategies the ones that can help you right now. Use these skills to augment your professional abilities, connect with the teaching community around you, and make your work of nurturing young people more of what you'd really like it to be. That's teacher empowerment, and you can make it work for *you*.

Acknowledgments

It has been our great fortune to talk with inspiring teachers and principals every day. Some of them are former students; others have taught in high schools with us; others work in schools that are part of the network with which we've been involved. They work in public and private schools, in-district and charter schools, urban and suburban schools, and elementary and high schools, both small and large. They are constantly studying new ways to reach their students, to work productively with their colleagues and administrators, to transform their schools into true learning communities, and to use their talents as fully as possible to cultivate their students' success.

We are extremely grateful to all of these educators who have taken time from their already hectic days to tell us their stories and describe their strategies for building teacher power. This book could not have been written without them. So our deepest thanks to Monty Adams, Xian Barrett, Lori Birenberg, Tina Boyer-Brown, Chip Brady, Stacy Buehler, Theresa Cameron, Khara Criswell, Kristi Eilers, Megan Faurot, Sarah Giddings, Janine Givens-Belsley, Maia Golley, John Henry, Jeff Hoyer, Lisa Kenner, Jill Knopic, Lorena Kramer, Mark Larson, David Levine, Ignacio Lopez, Aleks Mironchuk, Melissa Resh, Justina Rewilak, Evan Roberts, Amy Rome, Juli Ross, Karen Sabaka, Maya Sadder, Jim Schwartz, Allison Slade, Marilyn Strojny, Mary Beth Werner, Sharon West, and Tamara Witzl.

We are also grateful to the many educators both inside and outside of P–12 schools who have nurtured our thinking and given us academic homes. National College of Education deans Alison Hilsabeck and Jerry Ligon, the

Department of Secondary Education, and the president and provost at National-Louis University have been wonderfully supportive, and conversations with teacher-scholars from all over the university have been inspiring. Harry has been nurtured by the many conversations with his colleagues at Northwestern, particularly Louise Love, Jock McLane, Jim O'Laughlin, and Carl Smith. Sybil Dunbar modeled for him teacher power through intellectual commitment. Much of what he knows about high school teaching he learned from the inimitable Fred Schenck. The English department at Lake Forest High School demonstrated how much better we all teach with a community supporting us. And he has witnessed what it takes to nurture a vibrant school culture from working with the marvelous teachers and directors at Baker Demonstration School.

Steve has valued the long support and association of many friends and colleagues at National-Louis University. John Ayers and Pam Clarke taught him much when the three worked together at Leadership for Quality Education in Chicago. Elizabeth Evans, director of the Illinois Network of Charter Schools, and Hoy McConnell at Business and Professional People for the Public Interest have been steadfast supporters of this work. The talented teacher leaders in the Illinois Writing Project have demonstrated again and again what thoughtful and courageous leadership really means. The great teachers who founded and developed the Best Practice High School with him made teacher power a remarkable reality for him to see. And the many teachers and leaders in the Chicago Schools Alliance together delved deeply into the issues and challenges of distributing leadership and bringing sustainability to their innovative work with children.

Both of us have been fortunate to have Harvey Daniels and Marilyn Bizar as mentors, coworkers, and friends. We are especially indebted to Kim Zalent, at Business and Professional People for the Public Interest, for showing us how to help teachers speak up strategically and enable administrators to listen more to teachers' voices and respect them. And the administrators and teachers at a long list of schools have done much to shape our thinking about what teacher leadership means, even if they are not mentioned in the book; we hesitate to try listing them all for fear of forgetting someone important.

We've both been nurtured by the canoe trips and conversations with our men's group, even though we suspect that some of them would rather have dental work than hear anything more about the challenges of education. Harry also thanks graduate assistants Sarah Frost and Sarah Saghir for their invaluable assistance, and Wilma Stiltz for her great spirits and help around the office with anything that needed to be done.

Leigh Peake, now at Corwin Press, had the foresight to first encourage the creation of this book. And our editors at Heinemann—especially Lisa Luedeke and Sonja Chapman—have provided invaluable editorial guidance to make this book far better than the drafts we first sent them.

Our families come first, even if we name them last: Harry's: Heather, Madeleine, and Claire; and Steve's: Susan, Mark, and Dan. They give us great ideas, inspire and encourage us, listen to our complaints, and forgive our late return from long meetings.

Introduction: Leadership as Everyday Participation in Your School's Professional Community

Jill's Story

Jill, a fourth-year French teacher, garnered rave reviews from her supervisors for her teaching during her internship and was accordingly offered a teaching position at a prestigious high school in a prosperous suburb. Because of the parents' affluence, the school was shielded from many of the excesses of No Child Left Behind, including the preoccupation with test scores. Jill could not wait to use her best-practice communicative language teaching skills with the highly motivated students. Jill's department chair, however, was one of the few left from the "old school." She had no patience with Jill's Total Physical Response instructional methods and insisted that Jill stick to the textbook, drilling students on grammar rules and vocabulary.

Jill felt more and more isolated, despite the many great teachers in other departments throughout the high school, and her students, sensing that she was not teaching what she believed in, lost faith in her, too. When Jill's chair observed her in the spring, she criticized her for her lack of classroom management, and not surprisingly, Jill was told that she would not be asked back. We wondered: Might Jill have survived and prospered if she had developed some basic skills for connecting with other more supportive teachers? Sybil shows how this can happen.

Sybil's Story

Sybil, a chemistry teacher who graduated with Jill from the same preservice program, faced her own daunting trial when starting her career. She went straight to an urban high school with a population of high-poverty students, where the chair told her that even though she was by far the most proficient chemist at the school, she would have to teach physics, a field for which she was much less prepared. When she complained, her chair told her that her students wouldn't know the difference anyway because most of them would be lucky just to graduate from high school.

Though disappointed, Sybil approached a well-prepared physics teacher who taught during Sybil's prep period and asked about sitting in on the physics class for a term. She figured this was the best way to learn to teach physics under the circumstances. Sybil said, "I'll never be as good as this teacher is at teaching physics, because she has a passion for the field, but I learned a lot from her, and I don't feel bad because she'll never be as good as me at teaching chemistry."

Sybil also attended local teacher support groups in chemistry and physics and met university faculty members who helped her and her colleagues with innovative lessons and labs. She urged her most effective colleagues to stay at the school to help improve it, including an assistant principal who was offered a very attractive job elsewhere. She joined the technology committee, giving her access to new equipment and software, and volunteered to counsel the student peer mentoring committee, which helped her get to know her students.

Eventually, Sybil won the right to teach honors chemistry and started the very first Advanced Placement chemistry class at the school. Although still an untenured teacher and disliked—and perhaps envied—by her chair, she is admired by her colleagues and her principal. Sybil has developed a great reputation and has won grants and citywide awards, so the chair would not dare to terminate her contract. Unlike Jill, she loves her job and feels very supported at the school by many of her colleagues.

So What Do These Stories Tell Us About the Power Teachers Can Generate?

What is the difference between Jill's and Sybil's approaches? Jill thought that if she focused on being an excellent teacher—certainly a tough job by itself—it would be enough for her to succeed. By the middle of the year, however, Jill seemed to be burning out, even though she was still trying as often as possible to teach in the way she believed was most effective.

Sybil, on the other hand, has become even more enthusiastic about her mission because she treats her school as more than a collection of individual classrooms. Schools are complex organizations, in which our roles are determined not just by our training and expertise but also by many factors over which we do not have full control. However, we can achieve some *influence* over these factors, and by using this influence, we can not only become more effective in our classrooms but also help improve the entire school and feel much more job satisfaction—all without necessarily taking on formal leadership roles or becoming principals or superintendents.

This book, then, is about extending one's professional role in small ways and large in the school community, in order to improve one's teaching, one's work life, and the school as a whole—and that is what we mean by teacher empowerment and teacher leadership.

Does It Make a Difference?

We don't want to bore you with a long review of the research, but it is important to know that if you try some of the steps recommended in this book, it will make a difference for you, your kids, and the school. Here are some of the effects that have been observed:

- Distributing teacher leadership increases teacher effectiveness and student engagement (Leithwood and Jantzi 2000; Silins and Mulford 2002).

- Every Chicago small school that has improved student achievement shares *all* of the following features: (1) teachers work together regularly on common instructional issues; (2) the principal is deeply involved in initiating and supporting this work; and (3) teachers have influence on school policy and decision making (Stevens 2008).

- The extensive study *The Essential Supports for School Improvement*, by Penny Sebring and associates at the Consortium on Chicago School Research (2006), identified five characteristics of Chicago schools with the most improved test scores. One is leadership that includes teacher involvement and is focused on instruction. A second is a professional community committed to instructional innovation and to the school. Of course, safety, strong curriculum, and parent involvement also matter. But schools improved most when *all* factors were present.

● Contrary to popular belief, high teacher turnover is not so strongly related to working in high-poverty urban schools. Rather, limited input into school decision making is a major factor in teachers leaving their jobs, along with inadequate support from the school's administration, low salary, and student discipline problems (Ingersoll 2001).

As we suggest in this book, however, teachers need not *wait* for administrators to hand them more responsibility in order to make their jobs more fulfilling. Rather, we want to show you some ways you can do this yourself. So now let's define more explicitly what we mean by teacher leadership and teacher empowerment—and what we *don't* mean.

Everyone in a Teaching Community Actually Leads

Building teacher power involves taking responsibility, and that means becoming a leader in one way or another. But because of the way leadership works in many organizations—not just schools but banks, hospitals, and factories—most of us think of leadership in terms of people making big decisions, giving orders, evaluating subordinates, and perhaps occasionally whacking someone who isn't toeing the line. As a result, many teachers turn tail the moment they hear the word. Instead, we want to rethink the very idea of leadership to see how it can be something much more congenial and essential, a positive part of every professional life.

In fact, all of us exert leadership in one form or another all the time. It may be in a formal position or by way of informal relationships, influence with fellow teachers, or, very simply but importantly, by the example we set. Our actions always affect others and help set the tone of the school, and that is a type of leadership.

This kind of leadership may work positively or negatively. Maybe this doesn't happen in your school, but many of us have seen it: Somebody proposes a new idea in a meeting, and the school curmudgeon, who has no official leadership position whatsoever, offers a dozen reasons why it's no good. Everyone shuts down and the idea dies. That's still leadership, but it's negative leadership. Or there's the opposite: A highly respected veteran takes a new teacher under his wing or quietly gathers support for a new program, helping it spread across the school. The principal knows that this person's support can make all the difference in the success of a new program. That's leadership, too. In both cases, power derives not from any official authority, but from relationships, earned respect, and behavior patterns established over time.

Some education gurus use the term *distributed leadership*, which emphasizes shared responsibility throughout a school. And it reminds us that other adults in the building besides the teachers are also models and resources. A recent National Public Radio story featured a school maintenance worker who is also a poet and mentors kids throughout the school. To do this effectively, he and the official teachers have to coordinate their efforts and consult each other thoroughly, so that the poetry work fits in with the rest of the instruction taking place at the school. At Washington Irving School in Chicago, it was long a practice for students to approach any adult in the building to hold a conversation about the book they were reading and get a sign-off for their reading record. Lunchroom cooks were as helpful as anyone else, and so they needed to become an active part of the decision making about this program, along with the faculty.

Leadership, then, means taking a more active and constructive role in the professional community and developing an authentic kind of power that legitimizes and strengthens this role. All of us contribute to the culture of the school in one way or another, whether we are outspoken or silent. But what we're talking about is a more active and intentional approach to our role.

It's not about who a person is but what he does.

A better way to think about teacher leadership, then, is to recognize that, as expert Linda Lambert says, "leadership and leader are not the same" (1998, 8). We usually think of these two as synonymous, as if leadership is the monopoly of someone with a specific set of personal traits or a formal position. In this view, leadership belongs to a powerful personality with organizational authority to back her up. Either you've got it or you don't. But if, as Lambert explains, leadership is about thoughtful and strategic behaviors that help improve a school and increase kids' learning, then we can all exercise greater leadership and do so more intentionally—and that's the kind of leadership we're talking about.

So any teacher can take important actions like setting an example, sharing ideas to solve a problem in the school, asking for help, and building relationships. Each of us can find ways to investigate students' needs or try a new teaching strategy and share what we observe in a constructive and accessible way. If we do take on a more formal task, we can seek input and communicate about our work with as many colleagues as possible. Where conflicts or disagreements arise, we can seek ways to resolve them constructively. But doing these things well requires skills, and that's what we explore in this book.

One key element of such behavior is the building of *trust*. Much research suggests that schools don't improve unless the teachers have some colleagues they can trust (Bryk and Schneider 2002), so establishing this trust where it does not yet exist is a major contribution that is at the core of teacher power and leadership. It's a first step to entering more fully into the professional community. But this does not happen automatically. Teachers need to develop explicit communication skills—skills we can use, like how to sit down and find common ground with a colleague whose views of education differ from yours, or how to initiate a campaign for changing a school policy in a constructive way that is most likely to succeed. The challenges of educating today's changing student population cannot be met by a teacher-proof curriculum or a building full of disconnected classrooms. Improving schools in a more significant and long-lasting fashion will require this kind of in-depth work on teachers' part.

What about the differences between formal and informal leadership roles?

The number of formal positions for teachers has been increasing—including literacy and math coaches, lead teachers, and other coaching and mentoring positions. These have advantages and disadvantages. A coach has specific duties, time to do them, and perhaps some recognition for the work, but even if she just stepped out of the classroom a year or two earlier, teachers may see her as an outsider: "You don't have to face these kids the way *we* do every day!" But strategies for informal leadership can especially help a coach or lead teacher overcome the limits that a formal position brings with it. So we believe that formal leadership requires the same kinds of skills and strategies as the informal kind, only more so.

Individual or whole-school leadership?

We've described teacher power so far as mostly an individual contribution to the teacher community. Yet it's most powerful when the whole school embraces it. In a building where the principal promotes a professional community, the job of teaching is very naturally redefined to include responsibilities beyond the classroom (along with time and resources for them). Such a school has effective teams, well-designed professional learning, and processes that use teachers' expertise to make wise decisions and get everyone behind them. This makes it much easier for teachers to take on new roles and build leadership skills. Teacher power is something that grows; it's not just conferred. School climate and organizational structures can make a huge difference in supporting or neglecting teachers' wider roles, and we elaborate on this in the conclusion of this book.

BUT . . . there are plenty of schools where it's simply not happening. And there are more and more pressures from standardized tests, required goals, and lockstep curricula that appear to limit teachers' individual initiative. Teachers can feel helpless and isolated when they're under such pressures and lack real support. Sometimes they see their best efforts undermined by misguided mandates. Often, as a result, they withdraw into their classrooms and do the best they can. But that's just not as much fun. Even in the least hospitable settings, when individuals take small actions to improve their own practice, connect with others, and open their classroom doors, their work lives and teaching can get better and better. Perhaps the whole school doesn't change just yet. But teachers who are active and reach out discover a new sense of efficacy. They attract support from others who respond to their invitation. So, yes, a good school climate is important. But there's plenty that can be done, even when that's not perfect.

OK, so I'll be happier with my job if I exercise leadership. Is that it?

Exercising power in a teacher community is not just about being happier with our jobs, as necessary as that is for our own well-being and for a school to be successful. And it's not just about voting, or having a voice in decision making in a school, as important as those things may be. It's certainly not about maintaining the status quo. Rather, it's got to be about taking active responsibility—not just in your own classroom but also in the wider professional community of your school—for making learning deeper and more powerful for children. That's our core focus. Otherwise, we'd be forgetting the essential purpose—and satisfaction—of our work.

What This Book Invites You to Do

The thirteen steps in this book offer a variety of ways in which you can expand your scope, build your leadership capacity, and participate more fully in the professional community of your school. Some steps are small and easy to take.

These build to larger, wider efforts that involve more planning and time. We encourage you to start with yourself. As you become progressively stronger and more knowledgeable in your work, you can move outward to learn more about your students, connect with colleagues, engage in the professional life of the school, and finally connect with and draw in resources from beyond your building.

Following is a summary of the steps you'll find in this book.

Start with yourself.

In every profession—just as with ours—continually adding to one's knowledge and capacity is part of the definition of what it means to be a professional. By starting with yourself, you increase your own confidence and develop more knowledge that you can share when it becomes appropriate. If you are exploring an idea or activity you are passionate about, not only will you be energized, but that will sooner or later communicate itself to your students and your colleagues. One of the challenges of teaching is that there's no real career ladder, except for the one that takes you out of the classroom and into administrative and supervisory work. Therefore, if you intend to keep on teaching and working with kids every day, it's especially important over time to keep developing new approaches to your teaching and your work life so you don't grow stale or bored.

Understand the kids more deeply.

Developing teacher power and leadership is important *for your classroom*. Observing students and analyzing their work and their needs will of course make your teaching more effective. But when you begin to compare your observations with others', or work together on a study of student performance, you will move into closer collaboration with colleagues, which in turn will result in still more productive and creative lessons. Further, you can apply with students many of the same strategies you use when working with colleagues. Our students need to learn leadership skills as well—essential social skills of democracy, group work, teaming, and civic engagement—so you'll see an "In the Classroom" section in each chapter of this book. Finally, the kids will also learn from watching you, their role model, collaborate with fellow teachers and administrators.

Connect with fellow teachers.

Connecting with colleagues will enable you to avoid the isolation that can be so discouraging and limiting to the professional growth of individuals and the school. Strong relationships will make your work atmosphere more collegial and enjoyable. Even if your school harbors some apathetic or curmudgeonly people, you can still create a community where they have less influence over your work. Reaching out can be contagious. Teachers begin to help each other more, increasing the professional skills of the good ones and strengthening the weaker ones. More teachers will be working toward the same goals. If you've been feeling lonely doing high-quality, best-practice work, you can develop strategies for enlisting more support.

Take action in your building.

This means getting involved in a more intentional way—speaking out when that will help and initiating or contributing to efforts that can improve the school more widely. This matters both for you and for the school. For one thing, it's good for your health and happiness. Even if not all your efforts succeed, you won't feel helpless or victimized, so you'll be less likely to burn out. You'll achieve more of a sense of control over your work life and environment. And your involvement is needed for the school. If administrators are the only ones focused on school improvement, it's never going to happen more than superficially. Once the present regime moves on, improvements will evaporate if not sustained by a collegial learning community. In contrast, when it spreads to the whole school, teacher power means that school improvement is more than the sum of individual efforts. The whole school culture can become a trusting environment to which all contribute. This in turn builds *internal accountability*, that is, people committed to doing a good job for the kids and for one another, as opposed to *external accountability*, which is about people monitoring you, and which is far less effective.

Reach outside.

When you reach out to people beyond the school building, you'll have more resources to improve your students' education and your school. Parents become partners instead of griping adversaries to be kept at bay. Grants enable you to develop new projects that excite you and your kids. Partnerships with community organizations, businesses, or universities bring in specialized expertise and activities that both you and the students can learn from. Connecting with the wider community goes beyond just making use of its resources. A significant part of teacher leadership and power is coming to see yourself in a larger arena, a wider setting that includes not just your school and district but the community in which they exist. That community, and its social capital (or lack of it), has a lot to do with the conditions and character of your school, so you need to be in touch with it, work with it, and learn about it. And those parents and partners will in turn learn from you.

A New Professionalism

Teaching has always been a profession and not just a job. Whatever the rest of the world may think, the task of guiding students to conceive new ideas, understandings, and abilities is a complex one that, at its best, requires skill, experience, thought, artfulness, judgment, and many kinds of knowledge. But now, as it becomes clear that the external forces like No Child Left Behind are very limited in how much they can improve education in this country, the spotlight comes back to us, the teachers. In many schools and communities, kids really do need more than their schools have provided for them in the past. Yet we can't achieve that only by bearing down harder in our own classrooms. It's time for a new professionalism in which educators learn ways to work together more effectively. In some schools, they are already doing that, and we can all learn from them, as we will in this book.

At the same time, there's also a personal side to this new professionalism. Building a professional community can encourage you and your colleagues to stay in teaching as a career because the job becomes more satisfying in all sorts of ways, including offering the potential of monetary rewards and recognition beyond your district. But even if these kinds of rewards don't mean a lot to you, we hope the many teacher stories in this book will convince you that creating a warm and trusting professional community where the work you do is valued and respected repays many times over the efforts needed to develop this kind of workplace.

Hard Work, Low Pay, Scant Recognition

Good teachers know that making their classroom a great place for learning is job one, and it's huge and exhausting. We readily admit that at our stage of life, we the authors probably couldn't find the energy to do it! So then, who wants to take on more work and responsibility when we're underpaid, underrecognized, and overworked already? Compared with higher-paid professions, even the best-salaried teachers are hardly paid what they're really worth. Further, only a few school districts around the country actually have systems for fairly and constructively recognizing the higher levels of expertise and effort involved in teacher leadership. So it's no surprise that many teachers hesitate to do more than meet the direct needs of their students and the requirements of their contract.

Getting Over It

When we asked Karen Sabaka at Telpochcalli School in Chicago what she gets out of her leadership work, she listed a number of benefits. First, she remarked that she needed help to improve her practice, and many of the activities she initiated addressed that, particularly in literacy and bilingual education. Second, she approached co-teaching as an opportunity rather than an external obligation. While she did provide suggestions to her new teacher partner, she also set up occasions when they brought their two classes together so each received help and ideas from the other. Lastly, she admitted, "My friends and I are nerdy! We love talking about our work. I realize that not everyone is like that." At the same time, Karen realistically acknowledged that teachers who are raising young kids while guiding thirty more at school every day may not have the time that she does, so life stages can make a difference. So we show in this book how teachers can take small steps that contribute to their community and make their work lives more satisfying, even when major projects or big committee jobs are not within reach.

1 | Start with Yourself

How It Helps You

The American populace has a love-hate relationship with teachers. While most Americans admire and are grateful to their teachers, whenever anything is not going right in American education, it's convenient to blame those on the front lines. Too often, the supposed answer to any problem is either a teacher-proof curriculum or more outside testing to make sure that the teacher isn't goofing off. Fortunately, most teachers and plenty of appreciative parents and community members understand that teachers are our children's mentors and role models, and that in our twenty-first-century society, teachers are professionals and leaders who must apply their expertise and skills effectively for all children. Some of us, however, may feel so disrespected by either the children and adults in our schools or state or national policies inimical to teachers that we need to remind ourselves that we are professionals and leaders with significant power already. We have several suggestions for how to practice the conscious professionalism and leadership on your own that will help build your career, whether or not you ever take on a formal leadership position.

The place to start is with yourself and what you need in order to feel good about yourself as a teacher and a professional. Here is where Harry began:

> I entered teaching partly because I loved reading books myself and wanted to share this excitement with my kids—especially my love of ethnic and

international autobiography and memoir. However, I found that I was devoting all my time to planning, teaching, grading, and organizing the paperwork and was feeling more and more overwhelmed. I not only had no time to read but was becoming isolated and unfulfilled. Not surprisingly, I started to medicate my stress by munching between classes, which was easy to do because there was always a cornucopia of delicious treats in the teachers' lounge. At the same time, I rarely saw daylight because I arrived early and left late and could not possibly afford—or so I thought—to go outside during my one preparation period. As a result, I got no exercise and gained the freshman fifteen pounds. This of course made it harder for me to feel in control or handle my stress. Like many beginning teachers, I had not read any articles or books on professionalism or leadership in school, so I didn't know where to start.

So where do you start? Melissa Resh, as a first-year teacher at Young Women's Leadership Charter School in Chicago, found that professional reading was especially important for her. *Teaching to Change the World*, by Jeannie Oakes and Martin Lipton (2006), challenged her belief system. *Other People's Children*, by Lisa Delpit (1995), and Beverly Tatum's *Why Are All the Black Kids Sitting Together in the Cafeteria?* (2003) prodded her thinking about how she could connect with kids whose backgrounds were vastly different from hers. Reading books like these of course helps us become better teachers in the classroom. But this reading also stretches our thinking beyond the classroom. From the start, Melissa was beginning to consider how she could become a leader in the school and aid its success. So let's look at some of the many actions you can take to strengthen and deepen your own professionalism. While there are plenty of things you may choose to do that will contribute to the school and the teacher community within it, you need to be strong, confident, and knowledgeable yourself to build the basis for that work.

Make It Work

Start with your passions.

Whatever your passion—whether it's gardening, lacrosse, storytelling, computer games, forensics, cooking, blogging about sports or politics, following the most recent mathematical or scientific discoveries, woodworking, music, films, or reading in some particular genre like mystery or fantasy (all passions of teachers we know)—you'll become a better teacher when you incorporate that passion creatively in your teaching as well as in your outside life. In other words, your leadership will be most successful when it grows organically from what you enjoy rather than from something you do only because you think you should or because your principal wants you to.

Stay informed about your field.

Back in college, if you were like many education students, you joined the professional association in your field (National Council of Teachers of Mathematics, National Council for the Social Studies, International Reading Association, National Council of Teachers of English, etc.), but now perhaps you've stopped paying dues or reading its journals. It's time to rethink that. Belonging to one of these associations, reading at least a small number of tempting articles, and taking advantage of its workshops will repay the investment many times over. Sometimes the ideas may not speak to you, but then suddenly, as many teachers discover, you'll come across something that will change your entire teaching career. This happened for Steve when he first heard presentations on teaching writing by Donald Graves and Donald Murray, two of the greats in that field. Steve had struggled to help inner-city kids learn to write; from these two, he began to learn about the kinds of strategies that could truly open up possibilities for his students.

Expand on your knowledge and skills.

Now is a good time to reach outside your comfort zone and learn about areas that are new to you. Consider doing more to hone your own writing or technology skills, because these are not only crucial to our teaching but crafts on which we are often judged. Lack of skill with them can prevent us from feeling like—or being seen as—professionals and leaders. But also look for surprising possibilities or focus on your passions. Teachers in a number of Chicago elementary schools are learning to use the Responsive Classroom approach to deeply change how they talk and listen to their students and turn discipline challenges into occasions for social-emotional learning. At Al Raby High School for Community and Environment, teachers have learned GIS (geographic information systems), a computer technology that maps data in order to analyze community conditions and needs, and all their students now take courses on it as well. This not only keeps the synapses sparking in your brain but puts you in touch with what student learners are feeling and experiencing. And it widens your view of the possibilities for teaching and learning that you need in order to contribute to your profession.

In many states, there are now two or even three levels of teaching certification, from an initial to a professional or master certificate. To renew a certificate at the next higher level, teachers need to create and complete a professional development plan, which may involve taking graduate courses or choosing from a wide range of other professional development options to advance their career knowledge. Fortunately, these state requirements are usually written so that teachers can formulate their own goals and strategies. If you have to create a plan, why not take advantage of this opportunity to work on skills that may have grown rusty or get started on some of the many professional activities suggested throughout this book?

Model professional leadership.

Would you like to undo the more dehumanizing aspects of NCLB or a disrespectful parent, board member, or administrator? The first step is to remember why you became a teacher in the first place. Let people know, diplomatically, that we teachers deserve respect. In the classrooms or walking the halls, we need to think of ourselves as part owners of the building. That means we get to know as many people in the building as possible and avoid becoming cliquish. As the leadership writer Jeswald Salacuse writes in *Leading Leaders*, strong professionals think of themselves as "manager[s] of the education process in [their] organization" (2005, 133). They see students and parents as advisees and clients rather than subordinates or adversaries, and they are always reflecting on how they might improve their teaching, without being defensive or worrying that they aren't doing a good enough job. They are aware that both inside the classroom and throughout the building, they are constantly modeling leadership.

Document your practices.

Get it down on paper. Even keeping a very informal journal in which you write each day about particular students and events—and what you've done that was successful and fulfilling or not—can have a big impact on your teaching. Just as it is important to read your own choice of books and articles while your students read, keeping up your own writing is important modeling. It helps you unload stress, even though you thought you couldn't possibly have time to write. It's also a great activity to share with colleagues or a teacher group, especially if you haven't kept a journal before. Then you can gradually move from informal journaling to more structured documenting of how you've differentiated instruction, for example, or tried various strategies for reaching a struggling student. This is how many of us who write professional books got our authorial start.

Reflect on your teaching.

When you're jotting down a record of your work, it's pretty hard not to start reflecting on it. Especially if you are a fantastic teacher, you will be wondering what might make you even better. Inevitably, questions tickle at our brains. Do you suspect you've developed teaching habits you need to reexamine? Do you feel successful with some students but not others and don't want to just blame the ones who are struggling? Are the school's demographics changing, causing you to wonder how you should alter your teaching to reach your new students? Are you happy with your job, or is it less fulfilling than it used to be? Are you as efficient as you could be? Do you feel as if you're in (democratic) control of your classroom at most times? Might it help if you backward mapped your annual curriculum or even your units and individual lessons earlier? A strong leader is someone who is thoughtful and intentional about his actions, and that means looking back in order to become more strategic going forward.

Some teachers have decided that a smart way to document and reflect on their teaching is by studying for National Board Certification. The financial rewards can be ample: in Illinois, the state offers grants to pay most of the application fee, and in Chicago, Board Certified Teachers receive an extra three thousand dollars a year for ten years. Many schools are on the lookout to hire National Board Certified Teachers as mentors, and at this point, it's the highest official recognition for master teaching. It also fulfills state professional development requirements for earning a higher-level certificate. We know many teachers who say that though the application process is arduous, they learned a great deal from creating the classroom-based portfolio and studying for the exams. The five core propositions of the National Board for Professional Teaching Standards obviously reflect not only good teaching but also how to extend our professional abilities outward in our schools (www.nbpts.org):

1. Teachers are committed to students and their learning.
2. Teachers know the subjects they teach and how to teach those subjects to students.
3. Teachers are responsible for managing and monitoring student learning.
4. Teachers think systematically about their practice and learn from experience.
5. Teachers are members of learning communities.

Many of the strategies in this book will come in handy if you decide to apply for National Board Certification. We applaud initiatives to reward teaching professionalism and have more to say about reflecting on your teaching in Chapter 6.

Reflect on the school's mission and vision.

We notice in many schools that the principal often thinks the teachers are aware of the school's vision statement and core values and are on board, while the teachers either don't remember what the documents say, never knew, or just see them as a bunch of words. To make them really live, the entire staff, not just the principal or the board, should together revisit these documents every few years—to make sure that they accurately reflect the school's present status. Of course, in some schools, the mission and vision are so vague and general as to carry little meaning. But it can strengthen your own sense of direction and your wider view of the school to reflect on what you and your fellow faculty members are trying to do that really matters to you and to the community around you.

Use your nonteaching skills.

Considering you need to be good at fifty jobs as a teacher, it may seem a little unfair to ask you to do still more, but it's easier than it sounds. You probably already have a variety of skills beyond teaching, and if you're a teacher, you enjoy mentoring kids. One of the most obvious ways to use your talents is by coaching or guiding a student team or club. Students will love that you play guitar or soccer (even if not brilliantly), and there is nothing more freeing than working on a nonacademic task with children who are completely motivated. It also makes you more indispensable and can even make you unique. This is the kind of duty you may feel you don't have time for, but it will likely make you feel more fulfilled and will create energy, not deplete it.

Be resourceful.

It always surprises adults in the general public to discover how many job titles are actually subsumed under the title of teacher. They include business manager, saleswoman, writer and editor, interior decorator, marketer, social worker, trainer, political leader, handyman, coach, bookkeeper, referee, and many more. Now add scavenger to the list. Good teachers find all sorts of materials, gadgets, furniture, websites, strategies, games, and procedures to make their classrooms, their kids' learning, and their work lives more productive and more, well, fun. Being a professional and building your power and effectiveness means pulling in cool and useful resources from just about anywhere. Steve recently sat in on a math department meeting at which intense work was concluded with an old family-travel-in-the-car game called "buzz" that one teacher had remembered (Harry's family always played it on trips, it turns out). People stood in a circle, each counting a successive number, except that whoever got to a number with a seven in it, or a multiple of seven, or with digits adding up to seven had to say "buzz." The group had to start over if anyone missed. Sounds easy, but it's not. And it's great for teaching multiplication in the classroom.

Stay healthy.

Our grandmothers were right. It is difficult to be at top effectiveness or have a healthy mind or spirit when you're physically unhealthy. Teachers are constantly exposed to thousands of germs and have little time to wash up during the day, so we all need to figure out how to protect ourselves. Many colleagues will have great suggestions (Harry's is antibacterial hand sanitizer and Airborne—"created by a former second-grade school teacher"). We also need to try to address addictions like smoking so that we have a fighting chance of staving off illness. However, for many the problem's not cigarettes but junk food. Unfortunately, there is a reason that you so often find doughnuts and pizza in the teachers' room: we all tend to self-medicate when under stress. Some of us cannot stop eating such snacks once we've started, so we just say no to all food that we don't bring to school ourselves, other than fresh fruit and vegetables. Going cold turkey is a lot easier than trying to decide how many

Krispy Kremes are too many and then promptly breaking your rule! You'll be amazed by how much healthier and less stressed you'll start to feel.

Then there's exercise and activating endorphins. Fortunately, newer generations of teachers seem to be better about this, perhaps because so many are accustomed to working out regularly at a gym. And the good news is that you can get paid for doing this as a teacher, even if you're an indifferent athlete, by coaching or whipping up interest in a sports club. Part of being a professional and a leader is having energy to spare, and this is one more example of how expending energy can replenish you.

Help yourself to be positive.

Everyone derives a bit of satisfaction from venting. This is necessary and fine up to a point, if you're complaining to a friend or family member. And much of our skepticism as teachers is a well-earned response to the endless parade of reforms that never go deep enough or include enough direction from and support for teachers, in so many schools. But beware of treating a colleague like your counselor or therapist, since it can come back to bite you and is bad for your own job enjoyment and your school. It can become unhealthy and can turn into excuse making, which keeps you from solving the problems you're rightly complaining about. Many teachers use journals to express their frustrations and then move on to find a constructive approach to their challenges. This helps them stay positive, and it lightens their mood and makes them feel calmer.

It's fine to *say* "be positive," of course, but how can you do it in the face of the many frustrations that teachers often confront? One tenacious friend of ours makes a habit, when dealing with difficult situations, of reviewing all the options and then working strategically on those that offer the best route to success. We've seen her help turn around some really grim scenarios. And though she doesn't always succeed, she doesn't assume things are impossible unless all the possibilities are exhausted. We're not asking you to be a Pollyanna. But we do know that the research on successful leaders shows that they tend to be people who are optimistic and who believe enough in the possibility of change that they exert the energy to make it happen.

So what happened to Harry? How did he become more of a leader and professional and less of an overwhelmed clock puncher? He started to investigate his kids' reading habits, likes, and dislikes to see how he could suggest reading that would motivate them. In some cases that meant scouring indexes, databases, and bookstores for particular combinations, like science fiction with military themes, or African American authors who deal with gay themes. It also meant figuring out who his students were through strategies like asking them to describe their average day outside of school, using surveys, scheduling reading workshops, collecting exit slips, holding reading conferences, and many more. He began to observe other teachers' classrooms and to become comfortable asking them to observe him, with particular aims in mind. He started grading student work with a group of teachers who could compare their methods and results and then standardize them. He joined the technology committee and won a large grant, started doing action research, and eventually presented findings to two conferences organized by his professional organization, the National Council of Teachers of English. He began in-line skating and biking after school, lost some weight, and started to enjoy teaching as he never had before. He became a much better teacher and launched himself on the path that has led to the university department chair position he holds today.

In the Classroom

Schools and classrooms. Teachers and kids. They each form communities, and in many essential ways their dynamics aren't all that different. They each have a leader trying to guide them. They each have groupings, some formal and some informal, that may get along with each other and work together well, or not. They each have norms, some named and some unspoken, that guide behavior. They each have conflicts, large or small, that need settling. The leader could try to make all this happen herself, but everyone would benefit from sharing the responsibility among the members. So think how we could give our students a head start by helping them develop some of the same leadership skills we are proposing for you. Here are a few ways we could reinforce these lessons for kids in order to help them succeed in the wider world.

Help students see themselves as leaders.

Start with letting students know that it is their school, by enacting leadership efforts such as writing letters to the principal about real issues and developments at the school and consciously teaching the students leadership skills. We can create a safe classroom in which students have the space to develop by modeling calm leadership and nonacceptance of bullying and harassment and teaching conflict resolution skills. Students will often appreciate learning these skills more than anything else you teach them. Facing History and Ourselves (www.facinghistory.org) is an example of a powerful program for helping older students take responsibility for speaking out when harassment, violence, or bigotry is on display. *Increase the Peace: A Program for Ending School Violence*, by Steven Gevinson, David Hammond, and Phil Thompson (2006), is an excellent resource for this work.

Guide students to become resourceful.

We don't often enough give students opportunities to take responsibility. James Stigler and James Hiebert highlighted this problem when they analyzed the Trends in International Mathematics and Science Study (TIMSS) in *The Teaching Gap* (1999). They found that we teachers end up doing too much of the work ourselves. We need to involve students more as classroom citizens: coaching other students, taking notes on a minilesson for the kids who are absent, greeting visitors to the classroom and explaining to them the lesson taking place, presenting solutions to classroom issues, and conducting class surveys. Just be sure to choose nonmenial tasks that will indeed stretch their resourcefulness.

Teach students how to be organized.

We have always been surprised by the lack of time spent on the essential skill of organization, outside of special education and remediation classes. More and more, we are realizing that a lack of organization is one of the key factors preventing students from being successful in school and that we cannot expect parents and guardians alone to teach time management skills. In an age when some students have only an hour a night for homework because of after-school activities, and many others watch television five hours a night, schools are adding instruction in these areas. Many high schools are covering this topic in advisories, but it is probably taken more seriously when integrated into the regular graded course work.

Allow kids to demonstrate skills beyond the traditional ones.

Michael Smith and Jeffrey Wilhelm tell an important story in *Reading Don't Fix No Chevys* (2002) about an underperforming student who nevertheless was extremely skilled at fixing cars. Students like this, they found, do a lot more reading than teachers realize, though it isn't always the assigned reading for class. Many high school students who went on to become Olympic athletes and world-class musicians were not always the highest-performing students in the class. It is important to make room in all classrooms for students' real interests—and for us to bring our skills into class. As students, we ourselves were often mesmerized by teachers who were amateur musicians, actors, and dancers. One of Harry's elementary teachers was a principal singer in the New York City Opera. Harry didn't like him much as a teacher until one day he belted out the "Toreador's Song" from *Carmen*, at which point he became Harry's favorite!

Help students to stay physically healthy.

More and more schools are waking up to the importance of diet and its impact on student achievement. Pizza is being replaced by salad bars, and soda machines are being removed. Smart teachers include time for stretching, movement, and exercises that deliver to kids' brains the oxygen they need for thinking clearly. Physical education classes are becoming more useful for non-athletes as they mentor students on physical and spiritual wellness rather than focusing only on sports. Meanwhile, we need to be role models. We all know that we teach more through what we do than what we say, and what could be more persuasive than seeing us eating healthily and exercising every day?

WHAT PRINCIPALS CAN DO

Principals are increasingly under the gun to produce higher test scores among all groups of their students and are wondering, understandably, how teacher leadership should play out at their schools. In the end, the principals are held responsible for the success of their schools, so they naturally want to control the key decisions to ensure that success. But with all this pressure, what could be better than increasing a school's total capacity for change and bringing everybody on board the school-improvement train? Of course, everyone is focusing on reading and math. But to unlock more leadership power, principals should also investigate teachers' passions in gardening, music, film, computer graphics, or cooking. Look for ways that these energies can support the school's particular focus on improving student achievement, and encourage teachers to share these skills with their students and the entire school. Another strategy from our starting-with-yourself list is to bring teachers together for a day of strategic visioning—maybe a retreat in which the whole school writes up how the already written mission and vision could be reflected in individuals' and the school's core beliefs and actions.

In the 2003 "Metropolitan Life Survey of the American Teacher," about school leadership, teachers gave principals much lower marks than principals gave themselves in the areas of respect for and communication with teachers (specifically around a school's "instructional plan"), and "opportunities . . . to grow and develop," all of which teachers thought were critical (Markow and Scheer 2003). But strong principals we know make a point of helping teachers develop as leaders by offering opportunities to take on special projects and then meeting with them regularly to coach and guide their development. And the strategies that we're suggesting, like documenting and reflecting on their work as teachers, can be essential tools in this effort.

Understand the Kids More Deeply

Shadow a Student

2

How It Helps You

It's a great but all too rare learning experience to visit another teacher's classroom to see how a fellow professional does the job. We've noticed, though, that teachers making such visits often sit in the back of the room and watch the other teacher at work. We want to suggest something quite different, and teachers find it a real eye-opener: shadow a student and focus your attention *on that student*. Follow one kid for a chunk of the day—or all day, if possible. Sit next to her and periodically ask what she's doing and why. Get a sense of what learning is like from a *kid*'s point of view. *Don't watch the teacher; watch the kid and notice whatever she does*.

Why is it important? Very simply, to develop leadership and teacher power, teachers need to acquire a larger perspective—an understanding of the school, including how the students see it—instead of viewing the work only from our own desks.

We learned about shadowing as part of the Practice-Based Inquiry school visits designed by Tom Wilson, in Providence, Rhode Island, and used by the Chicago Schools Alliance, a network of Chicago schools we work with. The PBI visit, as we call it, involves a full-week observation of a school by a team of educators to provide in-depth, objective feedback to the school about how students are learning and how learning is supported at that school. Schools find the resulting reports extremely accurate and valuable for focusing on the most essential improvements they need to address. And the team members testify that the visits are the most powerful professional development they've ever experienced.

The PBI visit begins with daylong student shadowing by all team members. The object is not to evaluate individual teachers, but to see a wide swath of the school and how learning takes place for the kids. Teachers' awareness of their school is generally confined to their own classroom, plus what they learn from conversations with fellow teachers, and it understandably focuses on their own tasks. Rarely do we gain a broader picture of the school as a whole and what actually goes on in students' heads. Principals may seek more of this picture, but often their information is filtered as well. So to put it very simply: anyone attempting some effort, large or small, to improve a school or a classroom will be far more effective if he can see it in a larger perspective and understand its actual impact on kids.

Shadowing provides insights into student needs that you cannot gain any other way. After participating on one of the weeklong PBI visit teams, principal Allison Slade and first-grade teacher Maia Golley at Namaste Charter School in Chicago were inspired to have everyone at their small school experience shadowing for a day. When they compared notes afterward, the first thing the Namaste teachers all declared was that it was hard to sit all day. The school focuses on wellness, healthy diet, and physical activity, along with plenty of best-practice work on literacy and the rest of the curriculum. So it was a no-brainer first of all to add more physical movement to classes, using some of the Brain Gym activities (www.braingym.org) that help facilitate learning. The teachers went on to write individual reflections and to discuss their students as learners, writers, and mathematicians, and as students overall, drafting conclusions from their observations. We'll explain more about their other realizations in a moment.

Make It Work

You may want to start by just shadowing a student during a free period, which will only involve getting one other teacher's approval. Otherwise, setting up a shadowing process will take some arranging—a substitute or other coverage for your class, an OK from the principal and the teachers whose classrooms you'll visit. They'll want to know why you're doing this and will need reassurance that your focus will be on the student's learning, rather than on the teacher or her classroom methods.

We needn't give a lot of directions for this leadership activity beyond what we've already explained. Recruiting at least a few other teachers to take a turn at shadowing will make this a communal effort and increase the likelihood of follow-up action. Even if you can't include the entire faculty, getting one or two interested fellow teachers on board will galvanize energy around an improvement effort based on what you learn. If you must work alone, however, you are still setting an example, and other teachers are likely to be very curious to hear what you've learned.

When shadowing, it's crucial to stay focused on the student:

- What is the student learning?

- When is she paying attention (or not)?

- What is her experience of school?

- What does she think is the purpose for a particular task?

Sitting next to and at eye level with kids shows you the classroom from a new perspective. And often, little things go on in the back of the room that the teacher either cannot monitor, or chooses not to in order to keep the overall classroom activity going (with a last name starting with Z, Steve knew all about that as a kid). While you can't interrupt to ask the student her thoughts every other minute, at key points or at the start or end of a lesson you can find out what she thinks about the purpose or what she got out of it. Here are a couple of important questions to ask the student so you can learn about this:

- Tell me about what you are doing right now.

- Why is your teacher having you do this?

- What do you do if you need help or don't understand something?

- What have you been learning today?

Maia Golley remarked that you have to really discipline yourself to maintain focus on the student. It's natural for an observing teacher to watch the adult at the front of the room and make mental comparisons: "Well that's not how *I* would teach this lesson." But for this activity you must remain nonjudgmental (after all, you don't have all that much information about the context and what the teacher is dealing with) and instead find out as much as possible about what the student is learning. It's best, too, to avoid turning this into a search for deficits. Look for evidence of what the student is in fact learning, rather than what's not taking place.

Take time to process afterward.

Discussion about the implications (if you have some partners in this endeavor) is essential. Data gathering needs to have some outcome that makes a difference for your own teaching and for students' learning; otherwise, why do it? The simplest form of debriefing is just discussing with one partner what you've learned about how the student you've shadowed responds to the material being taught. You're bound to be enlightened by what you discover. When the Namaste teachers compared notes, they found, in addition to realizing how hard it was to sit still all day, another widely shared phenomenon: kids who were asked about the purpose for a task, or what had been learned during the day, could rarely give an answer. This was quite surprising to this group of smart teachers who had been honing best practices and seeing great results. It led teachers like Maia Golley to plan more discussion with the children about the purposes for her activities. "I want children to construct meaning for themselves," she explained, "but we also need to talk about it together." She added that this has forced her to clarify these purposes more fully in her own mind: "I needed to be much clearer about how I was using our time in the classroom." At the end of a lesson now, Maia writes "I can . . . " statements on the board with her students to help them reflect on their learning.

High school teachers are just as often surprised, after observing students in their colleagues' classrooms, by how little students realize why they are studying particular material. One teacher we know determined to ask students at the end of class to explain what they had learned that day and why it was useful. He was gratified to discover that students who did this were much more likely to think the class had been worthwhile.

At Harry's university, shadowing has long been a requirement for aspiring education students, several terms before student teaching. When they write about this experience, students invariably note with dismay not only the hard, cramped seats, but also how incidental the teachers sometimes seemed to the kids' day. Interactions with their friends during classes as well as in passing periods formed a large part of the students' experience. In their reflection papers, the university students write that this makes them more aware of the need to avoid overlecturing, to get students into groups strategically, and to be aware of the dynamics of student groups in various classes and activities during the day.

In the Classroom

Having kids visit classes in other grades, just as you will be doing, is an engaging strategy for increasing their awareness of what and why they are learning. Older kids can visit the classrooms of younger ones. Second graders can visit third grade near the end of the year to see what school will be like the next fall. As with the teachers' shadowing, the kids can gain a valuable perspective by pairing up with students in the host classroom and observing them as they work. The visitors can write about what it will be like to be a year older and learning about new topics and ideas—or about how they've grown, if they're looking back. And they will feel important, especially when visiting younger grades; we've often seen the most squirrelly teenagers go into total adult mode around younger children. In other words, they are beginning to see themselves as leaders.

Shadowing a teacher, principal, or other working adult can be even more powerful. After all, students rarely have a sense of what anyone other than their parents and one or two family friends or relatives actually does at work—if they even know that. They also don't do much reading about what people actually do in their jobs, even when they're in high school or college, though if they did, it wouldn't mean as much just to read about it. That's why so many high school and college graduates choose careers based on insufficient information or random job leads. Setting up this kind of job shadowing will obviously take some arranging with a host organization—a partnership effort that we discuss later in this book. Still, it's worth the effort. As part of his senior project in high school, Harry and a friend separately shadowed an English teacher at another friend's high school part-time for several months. Eventually, with the approval of the school, the teacher let Harry teach a couple of classes—two he remembers were on Wordsworth and the Book of Genesis—and Harry was hooked on teaching for life.

WHAT PRINCIPALS CAN DO

Every principal needs a clear picture of the learning going on in her school and should periodically take the time to do some shadowing. It won't be easy to claim large chunks of time for this, but we promise that the payoff will be much greater than it is from the interminable meetings outside the building. And remember, shadowing is not the same as observing and evaluating teachers, so it will be essential to make clear to the faculty that this is not just a stealth evaluation of their effectiveness.

It may also take some discipline to really maintain a focus on the kid, remain nonjudgmental about the teachers, and get the faculty to trust that this is about the kids' experience. One way to achieve this is to institute a program in which the principal and a number of teachers are all shadowing kids and then discussing the observations together. The principal is then joining more fully in the building's professional community. This is exactly what Maia Golley's principal, Allison Slade, did when carrying out the shadowing project at Namaste School, and that's why the teachers were willing to trust her enough to make themselves vulnerable—and to learn about how to become a better school in the process.

Look Inside
the Black Box

3

How It Helps You

College students who aspire to teach but have not spent time in schools sometimes think teaching ability is something you're either born with or aren't. What they and most members of the public don't realize is that teachers are practicing scholars who look inside the black box, studying the craft of teaching almost every day and often late into the night to improve their skills. Just think about some of the ways that you, as a teacher, practice scholarship. Even when you're not thinking of yourself as a researcher, you are mentally investigating your effectiveness at increasing student learning—comparing your success with different students, with different groups of students, and at different times of the day and year. You regularly collect evidence of student learning: reviewing class participation, homework, in-class work, performances, projects, quizzes, classroom tests, entrance and exit slips, and much, much more. So you're already spending many hours collecting piles of evidence or data, grading much of it, and using it to assess not only individual students but also the effectiveness of your teaching.

At the same time, you collect other types of evidence: You talk to colleagues on your team or in your department as well as other staff members—special education teachers, counselors, psychologists, deans, English language learning specialists, and the principal. You communicate with parents, researching what you can do with particular students or groups to improve their learning. You read as much as possible on the Web and in books and journals about ways to address your challenges and continue to improve your teaching. You try out solutions all the time, creating new lessons, units, and courses and experimenting with new methods for conveying difficult material and motivating students to love learning.

You may also gather information in workshops conducted by people from outside the school: writers on education, consultants, or university professors. In addition, you might attend state or national conferences, and perhaps you've led workshops for other teachers on your particular areas of expertise. Teachers are already scholars of teaching and are often more knowledgeable than the supposed experts who crisscross the country running workshops.

Do teacher research.

The next step for building teacher power in this area, then, is to become more organized and intentional about your inquiry process—getting some of the information down on paper, where you can analyze it to support or reject hypotheses about the effectiveness of your teaching decisions. In this way you can add to the growing knowledge about students and teaching in your school, for both yourself and your colleagues. You may even decide you are ready to share your investigation with others at a conference or in an education journal. Fortunately, many strategies for doing this work are fairly simple and will make teaching even more rewarding.

When we talk to expert teachers—those in the classroom or those who have moved into formal leadership positions—one common theme is their willingness to try out better strategies with their classes, share their results with colleagues, and keep trying new angles when one does not work out as they had hoped; that is, they are always actively researching. For example, almost all of Lorena Kramer's students at her large city high school were not making adequate yearly progress, so where could she begin? She first decided to tally her students' ten most commonly missed questions on assessments and address those deficiencies. Her math colleagues shared her optimism that this would work. However, as students' performance continued to flag, she concluded that it was "the wrong focus." So the next year she tried formulating graduated goals with each student, based on his initial assessments and the college-readiness standards from ACT and Illinois' Prairie State Achievement Examination (PSAE). This time, the students did much better, so she shared what she had discovered with her colleagues. Impressed, they adopted her approach, and she ended up becoming department chair and then math-science division head, where she has continued to research new strategies.

Conducting these experiments provided Lorena with the evidence she needed to make informed decisions about her teaching. In what other ways can purposefully looking into the black box help you?

It can prevent you from falling into ruts. Not only can classroom research suggest answers to teaching dilemmas, but it can also steer us away from continuing certain teaching habits just because we have always taught that way. Maybe those methods have lost their edge or were never that effective to begin with, or they might work in certain situations or with some types of students but not others. Janine, for example, who had always been an inspiring teacher, looked at her students' assessments and wondered whether she had been using her teaching time to maximum efficiency. So for summer reading, she investigated teaching "from bell to bell" and then tried out new techniques for beginning and ending her classes the following school year to maximize her students' time on task. She was surprised at how much the students improved and was pleased that reading up on a few simple strategies and then trying them out made such a difference.

It can help you differentiate instruction. Studying our teaching and our kids can be especially useful in figuring out how to help particular students who are difficult to reach with the methods that otherwise seem to work well. At Harry's university, during their internships, prospective teachers have to outline the strategies they are using with three particularly challenging students and document how these strategies affect students' academic growth.

It promotes professional growth. Investigating our work helps us reflect more purposefully and thus feel more in control of our teaching and more authoritative about our craft. Most of us experience this growth in knowledge each year for the first two or three years of our teaching, at least. Conducting even informal research can ensure the continuation of our intellectual development.

It can prepare you to explain and justify your teaching methods. Systematically observing teaching and learning makes it easier to discuss our goals and methods with students, parents, colleagues, and supervisors. It helps us develop a vocabulary to describe what we do. We're able to explain to ourselves and others how our teaching supports the school's vision and goals—a question that's becoming ever more frequent.

It can strengthen your leadership skills. Doing our own practical research strengthens our role in the professional community and our capacity for leadership, which, as in Lorena's case, can lead to new formal leadership roles. Even if we don't aspire to these formal roles, inquiring into our work represents a leadership skill that, just as in Lorena's case, ends up helping a whole department or school.

Make It Work

Most teachers already perform informal experiments and gather data to support or disprove their hypotheses every day. But the crucial next step is to document and become explicit about your hypotheses, research methods, and results, so you can share what you've discovered and help create a real dialogue on teaching in your school.

Here are five steps for looking into the black box and starting your own research project.

Start with a passion.

Choose a topic that motivates you, that gets you up in the morning. It might be the reason you decided to teach: to share a particular topic with others or to pass on to your students the joy that you received from one or more of your teachers. The best research often focuses on how to do a better job at giving students the skills to enjoy that passion as much as the teacher does.

Lorena's passion is making college possible for students who never thought they were higher-education material. This is an interest she developed while working at Saturn with teams of employees and watching how they all became energized to address the intellectual and practical challenges they faced.

Your project can start with a classroom challenge, but needn't do so; what is important is the passion. For example, Stacy Buehler, a preschool teacher, has been investigating the use of play to promote literacy. Stacy had always cared about the importance of play and is a wonderful singer of children's music—with two CDs to her credit and another on the way—so using play was already something she did well. But through her research, she's now learning more about how to run a classroom filled with play that seamlessly incorporates literacy development.

In other cases, your passion may coexist with a pressing teaching problem, as with a high school math teacher we know who was having trouble reaching his underprepared and math-phobic students. He wanted to learn how to empower them by placing math in a larger, less threatening context. He read Bob Moses and Charles Cobb's *Radical Equations: Civil Rights from Mississippi to the Algebra Project* (2002) and was so inspired that he began experimenting with algebra project strategies in all of his courses. Now his math classes are infused with social justice issues and are extremely popular with the students.

Think about your students.

What do you need to know about your students' lives — academic backgrounds, home lives, social groups, and cultural backgrounds? Sometimes we bang our heads against the wall trying to understand why we're not being successful with certain students, unaware that it's not about a lack of ability or effort from them or us, but just a shortage of information.

Researching and recording this kind of data, treated sensitively, can be an especially valuable project. At one elementary school in Chicago, virtually all the students are on free or reduced lunch, and a significant number are homeless. Students were often absent or tardy and were not making academic progress. The new principal, Amy Rome, in collaboration with most of the teachers, decided that the problem was a lack of information about the students and the challenges they faced. She and her faculty at first had no idea how to address such a large question, but with the help of one of Amy's graduate professors, Amy created a computer program that every teacher and staff member could use to document student dispositions and behavior.

Counselors, faculty, and staff regularly enter each student's most recent contact and family information and salient dispositional issues, which for many of these students change frequently. Cynthia, for example, may be focusing effectively in Ms. Jones' class but acting out in Mr. Washington's, and that may change several weeks later, perhaps as a result of a move or even a death in the family. Teachers contribute to this log regularly, typically between classes or before or after school. They share the information electronically or on paper with the student, staff, and parents or guardians when they come to the school (since most don't have access to computers). The emphasis is on creating information and support for the students. Teachers often catch students being particularly productive during a class and document that, even when the kids are not performing up to their potential in other settings.

Students can be given access to the information, and the families are shown solid evidence to help everyone make the right choices. Teachers find this system extremely useful, and indeed attendance has increased dramatically, and even tardiness has decreased, since no student can fall through the cracks. Test scores have increased as well, and in 2008, for the first time in the school's history, graduates were accepted at several highly selective high schools. Meanwhile, the school is collecting a treasure trove of data to help improve students' educational success. Professional development at the school often focuses on analyzing and acting upon findings from this data.

Read up.

Once you have a topic, do some reading, either on your own or, preferably, along with a colleague. The more motivating and enlightening the reading, the better. You may think this will take you away from your job and that you don't have the time, but it's another activity that will energize you and make you a better teacher.

Ask friends and colleagues about books that have changed their teaching or other aspects of their professional lives. We're not shy about asking the librarians at schools and at public and university libraries for suggestions, since that's a part of their job they enjoy. In fact, we have learned a lot from making friends with librarians and finding out their passions; they are a valuable and underutilized resource. It's also useful to scour the Web for articles in the teaching journals like *Social Studies and the Young Learner*, *Voices From the Middle*, and *Mathematics Teacher*. This is actually not a lot of work, and just a couple of hours can yield large rewards. The point is not necessarily to figure out exactly what form your research should take so much as to stimulate you and give you ideas. Reading with colleagues and talking the ideas over with them at school can be particularly fruitful and serve as a catalyst for a joint research project.

Figure out a research strategy.

You'll want your research to yield the types of answers you need and to document your findings. One useful method that doesn't take too much work is to code the questions and answers in the assessments you give, to reflect what you suspect but now want to document. Aleks Mironchuk, a high school math teacher, codes each question on her tests according to a college-readiness standard and then calculates the percentage of students who answer the questions in each area correctly. Analyzing the wrong answers also provides information about the ways students misunderstand the concepts she has taught. Then she is able to re-teach whatever is necessary, and can track students' mastery when a high percentage have correctly answered both lower- and higher-level questions on a topic. Aleks said that at first it was time-consuming to do this, but it was worth it because now she is no longer using on-the-fly perceptions to determine what students understand and where they are confused. And now her school has purchased a computer program that can do a lot of the busywork for her, but it wouldn't have made the buy without her and her colleagues' research.

Share your results.

Communicating with other teachers—one or two friends, or your grade-level team, committee, or department—can make things happen. As at Amy's and Aleks' schools, a whole department or a principal may become intrigued by a challenge or a research project and want to try it in many classrooms or throughout the school.

One great method practiced by many teachers is to have someone videotape your classroom when you are trying out an experiment and then discuss with a colleague (often the videographer) what she is seeing. Some departments review these videotapes together, because they involve flesh-and-blood students and provide plenty of raw material for fruitful discussion. More schools are also buying software to help to collect and analyze student information, which can be extremely helpful.

Some of the most interesting information can be obtained simply and quickly by two or more teachers looking at student work in a new way. Together, they review a sample of student essays, math problems, or artwork, not to focus on individual performance but on how effectively students as a whole are assimilating what is being taught and whether the material should be taught or graded differently. These artifacts can help guide a team or department to think through whether individual assignments are useful, how they should be graded, and what progress students are making. For this reason, more teachers are using portfolios that lay out each student's work as a whole. Once again, the key is not only to look over the material, but to summarize and reflect on it in writing. Many schools have started free Google groups or other online forums for this purpose, but you can start just by keeping the information in a file or on a personal computer.

While it is always rewarding to embark on a research project on our own, more often than not, word gets out and colleagues want to know more. For example, at an elementary school with an almost all-Latino student population, one teacher noticed that several of her new students seemed to have no knowledge of Spanish, even when their families were from Latin America. Some preliminary research on her students' language abilities showed that, as she suspected, a number spoke no Spanish. Since many classes at her school were taught in Spanish, she grew concerned and presented her findings to the faculty and staff with the argument that perhaps the school needed to further refine its dual language approach.

After a contentious but productive meeting, the whole school decided to embark on a short research project to determine whether this teacher's results were in fact representative. Several faculty members volunteered to collect each teacher's findings, and the technology teacher aggregated the data in an Excel spreadsheet. The faculty reviewed the chart and saw that the teacher who had raised the issue and one other just happened to have the few non-Spanish speakers in their classrooms, while the proportion in the rest of the school remained extremely low. The data and the spreadsheet produced a consensus that would never have been achieved by dueling stories. Meanwhile, the first teacher was commended for bringing this issue to everybody's attention and documenting her concern, and steps were taken to improve student orientation procedures for the minority of non-Spanish speakers who did need to be appropriately served.

Remember, to look into the black box you need not necessarily gather data in the form of numbers, use technology or the Web, or collaborate with others in order to investigate how to be most effective with your kids. The two most important steps are much easier to accomplish:

- *Expand the way you view your classroom.* Look at your students not just as individuals who have to learn in your class and be assessed, but as a group that can tell you more about student learning. View the work not just as evidence of each individual student's understanding, but as a larger set of data to be mined so you can become a better teacher.

- *Document and save.* It's good to get in the habit of documenting with a short commentary and saving the evidence you collect—in journals, charts, or any other form you'd like—so you can analyze it, share it, and compare it with later information.

In the Classroom

Just as teachers need to develop the habit of stepping back from their day-to-day work to think about and document their teaching, students need to develop similar metacognitive habits of mind. As we described in Chapter 2, teachers who shadow students often notice that kids seem unaware of why they are studying particular topics and what their learning goals should be. And it's hard for students to collaborate with their teachers when they don't know why they're even studying a particular piece of information or why they're using a particular method to learn it. So let's help them develop a research approach to their own learning—which means posing questions about important ideas and skills, and then pursuing learning in response to these questions.

Involve students actively in planning and reflecting on their work.

Even younger students can talk over and help define the learning objectives for a course and for individual units, as well as draw the connections between these objectives and particular topics and assignments. Students can also contribute regularly to their own assessments, submitting questions that assess specific learning objectives, whether it's understanding the economic causes of the Civil War or showing that they can use a scientific method to solve a problem. And when students write about their progress regularly, based on the evidence in a portfolio, they develop observational habits of mind.

Introduce problem-based learning.

Students pursue problem-based learning by working in small groups and exploring real-world issues with interdisciplinary elements rather than studying a preorganized textbook. It's a wonderful strategy that helps students learn to be researchers, but if you're thinking about trying it for the first time, it's wise to plan carefully to ensure students' success (helpful resources are available at the website of Samford University's Center for Teaching, Learning and Scholarship: www.samford.edu/ctls/). The kids will need to see examples of successful projects and get step-by-step help organizing their inquiry. Then, if you check your plan against district or state standards, you'll find it easier to justify to yourself and others the extended time that such projects take up. The professional text *Content-Area Writing*, which Steve coauthored (Daniels, Zemelman, and Steineke 2007), contains some good examples of various kinds of problem-based inquiry projects (see especially pp. 187–252).

Encourage research into new media.

Newer areas of study like media literacy provide perfect opportunities for students to examine the constant barrage of information they receive, conduct research on its veracity, and document the evidence of its purpose. That way, when it's time for them to complete more formal research projects, they can make the connection to the rest of their schoolwork and to their lives as thoughtful citizens, instead of just experiencing a boring, *sui generis* rite of passage. Then research projects will be just slightly expanded versions of work they've engaged in for years.

WHAT PRINCIPALS CAN DO

Schools that do the best job of supporting faculty research almost always meet four criteria:

1. Faculty are involved from the beginning in creating school-improvement goals instead of just being called in when it's time to "improve their teaching." Regular research and meeting time needs to be allocated during the school day, since conducting faculty research is considered a part of teachers' professional work life.

2. The principal makes clear the separation between faculty evaluation and the sharing of classroom research, so that teachers feel safe sharing sensitive information from tests and performance assessments. They cannot be worrying that they have to defend their performance while at the same time reflecting objectively on their own and their colleagues' practices.

3. Specific research projects related to the school's strategic plan are focused and short-term to prevent burn-out and to promote a sense of achievement for the hard work involved. Time lines for projects are relatively detailed, while still somewhat flexible, to meet longer-term goals and avoid later misunderstanding.

4. When considering school improvement projects, no ideas are rejected out of hand as beyond the realm of possibility. Investigation and carefully

documented pilot projects—that is, research—can help everyone to make a well-informed decision before taking a big leap. We know of schools that have radically and successfully altered their daily schedules to allow for greater student learning and professional improvement, while others have become year-round or added summer school. These changes were not necessarily practical in the short term and often involved seeking new funding or parent and community approval. But they all started with people at the school asking probing questions, gathering data on similar efforts at other schools, and carefully evaluating the pros and cons so that everyone was well informed by the research before moving ahead.

Connect with Fellow Teachers

Open the Classroom Door

4

How It Helps You

No aspect of teaching is more debilitating for teachers than the isolation from other adults that is so often part of the job. Study after study shows that this side of teaching pushes out of the profession even those who love their students and are passionate about knowledge. It is also the aspect of teaching least understood by outsiders, including, unfortunately, many education leaders. How can a teacher feel isolated when she is surrounded every day by hundreds of children or adolescents, as well as teaching colleagues and staff? Even teachers themselves sometimes don't understand why they feel unfulfilled, and feel guilty that they experience this when they're supposed to love their kids so much. Could it indicate that they are not meant for this job?

What teachers who work in true learning communities realize is that to develop as an educator, one *needs* the kind of serious analysis of teaching that can occur only among colleagues. In many other countries, like Japan and Germany, *half* of a teacher's day is devoted to professional analysis and planning (Darling-Hammond 2005), but here in the United States, teaching has traditionally been seen as a task someone can perform intuitively. Further, in many schools, teachers' planning time is completely taken up with other responsibilities like lunchroom, hall duty, or test monitoring, and even lunch is a rushed affair of twenty minutes or less, sometimes spent making small talk, and other times gobbled up while tutoring students. Only teachers know how exhausting it can be to do an intellectual job involving as many as a thousand interpersonal exchanges and scores of decisions (Jackson 1993, 11) each day with so little time carved out for reflection. Even in the evening, reflection has to fit in between grading, planning, reading, and family activities, and if it's to take place with others, it will have to be on the Internet in the chat group set up for the school's faculty.

So a crucial step in developing teacher power and advancing your career is to connect with other teachers. But not just any sort of connection. Recent studies have shown that teachers in Chicago small schools are more supportive of one another than those in larger, traditional schools, but much of the talk is about incidentals and logistics like managing the schedule for the computer lab or finding where the classroom sets of novels are stored (Stevens 2006). What teachers need as professionals is to talk about the things that matter most for their kids' learning, to exchange ideas and experiences and philosophies about their practice. Initiating this exchange with others in your building is a powerful leadership act, and it needn't take a lot of time or planning. An energizing and productive way to begin is by opening up classroom doors, visiting other teachers' rooms, inviting them into yours, and having conversations about what you and they see.

Here's how it helps one teacher. Monty Adams, who teaches high school science, keeps his ears open for anybody carrying on interesting work in classes: "If I hear somebody's doing something I want to do or I learn that they're dealing well with discipline, I'll stick my head in, even if for a short time." Monty also tries to encourage other teachers to collaborate with him, so if he's in the library having students do science research, he'll ask colleagues in English who've brought classes there if they'll take a few moments to help his kids with writing their reports. He did this so regularly that it led to collaboration with a couple of English teachers about better integrating their subjects. While the teachers couldn't arrange actual co-teaching, they figured out that Monty was teaching evolution just when the English teachers were on *Inherit the Wind*, about the Scopes trial. The English teachers had been stymied when the students didn't understand the play's scientific context, but with a few planning sessions, they modified schedules to build in references to each other's units and create the beginnings of an interdisciplinary project. Monty enjoyed the intellectual challenge, and just as important, the teachers made some headway against the fragmentary curriculum that trips up so many underperforming students at large suburban high schools.

Monty also welcomes observations by school visitors and lets the front office know that unlike many of his colleagues, he wants people to see his classroom: "I get a lot of curriculum ideas from visitors from different types of public schools." They ask questions that encourage him to explain why he uses certain strategies and thus to reflect on what he might do differently.

Make It Work: Classroom Visits and Peer Observation

Increasing numbers of schools have recognized the value of peer observation for retaining teachers, improving the school, and reaching every student, including those whose many challenges need to be nurtured by a team. But of course the devil is in the details. When Aleks first came to a large urban high school, the administration had, in fact, instituted a policy of regular peer observations. The problem was that teacher-observers had to share their reports not only with the observed colleague but also with the principal. Naturally, the process became just another meaningless task, with no one willing to betray peers by honestly commenting on the characteristics of the teaching she'd seen. Fortunately, Aleks' department chair campaigned to have the reports shared only within the pairs. Another change the chair made was for the observer and the observed teacher to decide on the particular objective of each observation beforehand to make the activity more focused and useful.

If you are interested in peer observation, it's helpful to consider the following.

Start out gently.

In schools that lack any tradition of peer observation or sharing, people may be slow to open up to this process, or even if they allow it, they may say nothing probing or critical, to avoid appearing as if they think they are better than their colleagues. This is a strong and historic norm in many schools. One way to get started is with cross-classroom visits that take place *after* school. The conversation, then, is about artifacts in the room—stuff on the walls, books, the furniture arrangement, student work posted or stacked on a table or tucked into portfolios. It's not as threatening for the host, but the conversation can still be productive.

For Juli Ross, a fourth-grade teacher (and no relation to Harry), the key is not formal observation, which can so often be bureaucratic, but collaboration. This whole book is in fact about the collaboration that is an essential component of teacher leadership. Observation, as Juli pointed out, is just the most basic form of collaboration: "Even if I'm supposed to be observed formally, I like to offer to have the observer teach with me. Then I'm learning from the other teacher's style. We have always talked about spending a day each quarter teaching in other people's rooms. Well last year we made a commitment, and I taught with Jen in her classroom. Jackie and I also teach together a lot."

Give yourself time to get used to it.

Even teachers who long for a connection to their comrades may need some adjustment time. One teacher we know arrived at a new high school to find the department working as a family, with a common room and writing lab that everyone used as a joint office during prep periods. But the most important difference was their tradition of observing each other teach. At first he found it off-putting that other teachers could just walk into his room, his private castle. He would let down the drawbridge when being evaluated, of course, in which case he would spend extra hours planning the best possible show—with great anxiety, we might add. But he was much too worried about being judged, even though he thought of himself as a good teacher, to open himself up to observation by his peers when it wasn't required.

Slowly, he told us, his attitude began to change, as those observing him showed no propensity to criticize but in fact suggested all sorts of useful strategies and lesson ideas. Occasionally an offhand comment made in good faith still rankled; for example, had he noticed that the group in the back of the room was not on task? The other problem was that even at this school, where the department and even the whole school felt like a family, there was no formal observation policy, so some teachers could still opt out, and the reporting-out mechanisms were all informal and up to individuals. Time was also an issue, and sometimes it was hard to justify going to observe a class when he hadn't even prepared his own next class. Nevertheless, it was great fun to have someone run into the writing lab or his room during a prep period to announce, "Matt is doing his cool lesson on the *Wizard of Oz* using Pink Floyd's *Dark Side of the Moon*. Want to come watch with me?" or "Mark is doing a war games simulation in his class; let's go." No longer was teaching an isolated endeavor whose victories our friend had to depend on his wife to approve; meanwhile, he was becoming a better teacher just by virtue of thinking more consciously about every strategy and lesson that he taught.

If your school doesn't encourage peer observation, mentor a student teacher.

Even schools that don't make a practice of observing usually take on student teachers, and becoming a cooperating teacher who mentors an aspiring candidate can be a great way to revitalize one's teaching. Even though the student teacher may be unaccomplished or unprepared (within limits, of course), mentoring can lead one to reflect on long-standing teaching practices that may benefit from adjustment.

Sybil, whom we described in our introduction, was impressed by how her student teacher interacted with her students. "I sat in on her class many times to see how she interacted with the kids. Kids I had trouble with she did well with. She did little cutesy things that they liked, treating them as a little bit younger, which I had always avoided. But when the kids talked about her classes and how much they enjoyed them, I knew what they were talking about." Sybil feels she was a good mentor to her student teachers: "I helped them to become more reflective on their teaching and showed them how to let students evaluate them and to allow students to be critical of them without being defensive." But she also made subtle adjustments as a result of what she learned and acknowledged her indebtedness to them for improving her teaching: "Any time you're teamed, you both can learn from each other. I wish we could do more of it."

Mentor a new teacher.

Whether it's part of a formal program or an effort of your own, mentoring a colleague is complex work that takes time and thought, so it's likely to be more involved than the strategies we've described thus far. And it's a role you will probably decide to take on only if you've racked up enough experience to feel confident of your ability to help. On the other hand, it can be not only a help to a new teacher in your school but also a key step in building your own professional power. Especially for teachers with many years of experience, one satisfaction in the later stages of our careers is to share our wisdom so that younger colleagues can succeed more quickly and avoid some of the pitfalls that we were not able to circumvent. Of course, this needs to take place in a sensitive and thoughtful manner. Steve still recalls a moment many years ago when, wrestling unsuccessfully with a mechanical task in his backyard, he finally turned to his neighbor, Mr. Bodo, who was sitting on his back porch.

The Closed Classroom Door

Let's face it: while we accept the occasional necessity of being evaluated, few people enjoy it. So if we think that being observed or asking experienced colleagues for help will lead us to be judged, most of us will avoid it. As Juli, who talked about collaboration, told us, because new teachers don't want to be vulnerable, "they say, 'I'm fine, I'm fine, I'm fine,' instead of 'I need help.'" Another reason teachers may lie low and avoid a wider arena is that it's a handy coping mechanism when faced with arbitrary mandates we don't believe in. Quiet resistance has enabled people to maintain a modicum of independence in many an organization. But there's a price. You're cut off from others, unable to get help when you need it or share wisdom when you've gained it. Your world is narrower. You may exchange gossip in the teachers' lounge, but you aren't really connected professionally. You're on your own.

Getting Over It

When Lori Birenberg started her teaching career at a large urban high school, she was nearly overwhelmed by her responsibilities, received no support, and saw no point in seeking any, since no one wanted to help. "It was toxic there," she recalled ruefully. Then she discovered an island of positive energy in the writing center run by Yolanda Simmons, who herself has gone on to become a published author and staff developer, focusing on literacy and family history. Lori explained,

> I'd go down to her room and cry every day. Well, I didn't cry that much. But we started having conversations about teaching. And we started putting kids' writing up on the walls outside our classrooms. The other teachers thought we were crazy—why would anyone do *that*?

Finding a friend made a huge difference. Nevertheless, understandably, Lori left after a few years to stretch her leadership talents. She helped to start a new small school and has been actively planning and teaching in such places ever since.

When Bodo offered a useful tip, Steve asked, "Why didn't you tell me sooner?" His neighbor, an HVAC contractor with many years' experience in coaching apprentices, replied, "I was waiting until you were ready to ask."

The importance of mentoring in teaching has long been recognized, but improvements in this area have accelerated over the past two decades. A survey in 2000 showed that 26 percent of teachers had served as mentors and 23 percent had received mentoring (National Center for Educational Statistics 2001). While not ideal percentages, the number of mentorships appears to be growing. No doubt some of this support was helpful and some not. A widely used approach, called cognitive coaching, developed by Art Costa and

Bob Garmston, deepens the mentoring process and ensures that it isn't just a charade or a relationship that ultimately disappoints. Even if the mentoring that you do is very informal, the concepts of cognitive coaching provide a valuable guide for your efforts by recognizing how change and growth actually take place for adults. The main principles are these:

- Build trust by developing physical and verbal rapport.

- Facilitate thinking through questioning and developing greater precision in language.

- Develop a person's autonomy and sense of community by increasing his sense of efficacy and self-awareness.

- Distinguish between coaching and evaluation.

- Rehearse coaching interactions that are congruent with a variety of styles.

- Apply coaching skills that enhance the intellectual processes of performance.

According to the Center for Cognitive Coaching, "In Cognitive Coaching, the person being coached, not the coach, evaluates what is good or poor, appropriate or inappropriate, effective or ineffective about his/her work" (www .cognitivecoaching.com). Karen Sabaka, an accomplished teacher whom we quoted in the introduction, approaches mentoring as a two-way street and finds she learns as much from a mentee as she gives.

Chip Brady, an experienced U.S. history teacher, has participated as both mentee and mentor in a long-running mentoring program at Evanston Township High School, north of Chicago. The program pairs experienced and newer faculty teaching the same course in side-by-side classrooms. The pairs plan lessons together and sometimes combine classes, allowing each to observe and give feedback to the other. They also grade some student papers together, which not only enables newer teachers to think through the evaluation process but reveals what students are learning, thus guiding the teachers' further instruction.

Chip understands the delicate balance involved in the coaching role, in part from his own two-years as a mentee, which he says "was the best experience for learning to teach that [he] ever had." He usually provides past lessons he has designed (or inherited himself) but then encourages his mentee to be creative and develop further on his or her own. A first-year teacher can be nearly overwhelmed with the work, however, so he doesn't hold back when more help is needed. He also especially emphasizes the observational side of the work. "It's almost impossible to really help a new teacher without seeing how he or she handles interactions and the various kinds of challenges that arise in the classroom." The history faculty at ETHS has come to value this program for the larger purpose of passing on important understandings about rigor and student engagement. So mentoring is about more than providing help for individuals; it's also about sustaining a school's instructional philosophy and goals over the long term.

In the Classroom

Can kids coach one another? Of course they can, but they need to learn how to do it effectively, just as adults do. Peer editing in classroom writing workshops offers a great setting for students to help each other, but many teachers worry about a number of potential challenges. For example, it's possible that the helper

- knows less than his partner and can't really help

- will hesitate to criticize for fear of hurting a friend's feelings

- will just go ahead and fix the writing, which won't really teach the writer anything

Here's how one fifth-grade teacher dealt with these concerns. When she held writing conferences with individual students, she had two or three others sit in on the conference. This enabled them to observe how the teacher offered guidance and to join the discussion. The teacher was skilled at posing nonjudgmental questions that drew out the kids' ideas and probed their authorial choices: "So what happened after you got home from the hospital?" and "You could start the story by complaining about your friends or by explaining the events. Talk to me about why you chose the first option."

Later in the period, when several students were acting as conferers, Steve observed one girl respond to a writer who had approached and asked her just to find the mistakes he'd made. "You have to tell me what kind of help you want first," she replied, urging him to take more responsibility and review his own writing first.

"How did you know to do that?" Steve asked her.

"We're experts in here," she explained.

WHAT PRINCIPALS CAN DO

Principals can support teachers' cross-classroom visits and mentoring efforts, but they need to structure guidance carefully so that it does not inadvertently undermine the very purpose—teachers learning from each other—that these activities are meant to serve.

- *Involve teachers in the planning*, so they have some input and start right off with some commitment and understanding of what and why this process is being undertaken.

- *Develop a culture of sharing* and providing constructive feedback gradually, so that teachers can grow to trust the process and experience its benefits.

- *Create a safe environment.* Both observers and observed need to operate in a safe setting in which honest responses can be given and received without threat.

- *Give teachers some measure of control.* Teachers who are being observed need to feel in control of the process and be able to determine what aspects of their practice they want to have examined. In fact, just as with student conferences, it's good to have a protocol in which the person being observed does much of the talking, explaining to her partner which aspects of the lesson she believes went well, what issues she's been working on with various students, and in what areas she'd like advice. On the Internet, the University of Texas at Austin has a handy guide for cognitive coaching that includes a thoughtful set of questions mentors can pose so that it's the observed teacher who does the talking and reflecting (go to https://uteach .utexas.edu/go/wings/Mentor-Development/; the questions can be found toward the end of the page on cognitive coaching).

- *Give teachers time.* If the only time available for observing or mentoring is during teachers' planning periods, it will be difficult to maintain the activity. One solution that costs a bit but needn't break the bank is to periodically hire a set of subs for the day and have them float from room to room to release each teacher for an hour's observation or mentoring meeting.

5 | Build Bridges

How It Helps You

We all know how to create relationships. We have close friends. We find fellow teachers we can talk with honestly about our victories and struggles. But what about faculty members with whom we are *not* well connected, perhaps because they work in a different department, grade level, or wing of the building, and we never see them? Perhaps they have philosophies of teaching different from our own, or their job simply involves a different focus and we end up competing for the same limited resources. Who wouldn't like to have some skills for settling a conflict amicably, rather than seeing it escalate, turn bitter, and make going to work more stressful? And wouldn't it be great not only to settle that conflict but to replace an unpleasant, combative pattern with an ongoing, trusting connection?

The most powerful tool for doing this important work is to have a discussion that can lead to a new or rebuilt professional relationship. This is a key step, as we shall see in many chapters of this book, for developing trust among colleagues, strengthening the school, and improving your work life, and it represents a true leadership act. Actually, even with colleagues we've known and appreciated for years, it may be surprising to find out, through a structured discussion process, sides of their thinking or experience that we'd never known. Community organizers view this kind of relationship building as essential to almost all their work. It establishes a basis of trust and understanding and enables them to identify the common interests around which people can solve problems, bridge differences, and get work done.

■ Make It Work: One-on-One Meetings

The one-on-one meeting or discussion is community organizers' strategy of choice for opening up possibilities with people who don't see eye to eye with us. Variations are also used by marketing firms to learn about people's deep feelings and beliefs and with consulting groups to solve problems in businesses. As explained to us by one organizer, a one-to-one relational meeting is

> an intentional, face to face, one to one meeting with another person to understand their interests, passions, and story, and to share your own—to explore trust with the other person and the possibility of a public relationship with them . . . so you can act together on issues of common concern. (handout by Nicholas Brunick, of Applegate and Thorne-Thomsen law firm)

What a one-on-one meeting is *not*:

- an opportunity to sell your ideas or to ask for help with a task or project

- an occasion for chitchat

- a search for someone who agrees with your point of view

- a search for friendship (Instead, it helps you build a *public* relationship, which is not the same as a *private* personal friendship.)

A one-on-one meeting provides an occasion to listen to and learn about another person's stories, insights, memories, and visions, while valuing that person's perspectives. It usually lasts just thirty to forty-five minutes and offers an opportunity to learn what makes that person tick, his priorities and self-interests, and how these came about. It's an exchange. You discuss some of your own experiences and beliefs as well as asking about his, without worrying about being a little nosy.

How do you start a one-on-one session? If you find it too risky to start right off with someone you are having a conflict with, then practice first on a friend. Whomever you are meeting with, though, it's a good idea first to clarify the purpose of the discussion. If, in fact, differences have existed between the two of you, your partner may be anticipating some agenda or argument, which is not what this session should be about. So you can explain and reassure:

> I know we've taken different points of view on some issues at our school. But I'd just like to know more about your background, so I can understand where you're coming from. And I'd like for you to learn more about my work experiences, too. This way we can see what goals we have in common as well as why we differ about some matters. I'm not asking for any particular action. I just think we'll be able to work together more easily if we know a little bit more about one another. This might seem a little unusual, but I read about it in a book on improving schools, and when I tried it with some teachers at my old school, it turned out to be pretty interesting.

Then, one good way to start is to say:

> One thing I'd like to learn more about is how you came to teaching in the first place.

After your partner has told his story for a few minutes, go ahead and share your own. You may be surprised at the similarities or connections that turn up—or be interested in the contrasts—and it's good to share your thoughts on these. You may well have a number of follow-up questions to ask as well. Another set of questions to pose is about the person's professional values:

> So what are some of the goals that are important to you in your work?

> I wonder whether any particular experiences led you to these goals.

When math teacher Jill Knopic, at Al Raby High School for Community and Environment, tried a one-on-one meeting with Tom O'Brien from the history department, she realized how little she had known about him. While they weren't actually adversaries, she'd wondered whether, as a Teach for America corps member, he was really committed to the profession or intending to leave after just a few years, as some TFA graduates do. This was especially important to her, since Al Raby faculty members are strongly committed to working together and making a difference in the community. Of course, she was happy to hear how much he did indeed care about this work. "I already had friends at Raby to turn to," Jill said, "but if I didn't, this would be a great way to help me make some connections."

Naturally, we also need conversations that aren't this structured. Seventh- and eighth-grade social studies teacher Janine Givens-Belsley engaged in regular talks with her grade-level partner, whose style and philosophy differed considerably from hers. He favored heavier discipline but actually structured his classroom activities much more loosely. Janine, on the other hand, preferred a tight classroom organization, with every step of the work clearly spelled out. Unlike her partner, her discipline style was to keep the kids busy and deal quietly after class with anyone who acted out. This difference caused a number of incidents and increasing tension between the two teachers. Janine, however, sensed that he was an interesting individual beyond his teacher persona, so in numerous lunchtime conversations, she did a lot of listening and tried to identify values they shared. "I knew we weren't going to agree on most things. He thought I was compulsive, but that was OK as long as he respected my needs. Sometimes his yelling, across the hall, disrupted my class. On several occasions he entered my classroom to round up the kids before I was finished with a lesson, and I had to draw a boundary on that. But give-and-take was important, so sometimes I'd let him take away my class time so he could give a test, even though I thought he really didn't need it." The two would never be best friends, but the frequent discussions led to compromises on both sides, defused tensions, and ended up creating mutual appreciation of each other's differences.

When It Gets Tougher

Sometimes the lines of force between two teachers in a school are like the north poles on a couple of magnets, repelling each other implacably—or so it might seem. Perhaps the school is divided by factions. Maybe teaching philosophies differ sharply. Perhaps some action or crisis has exacerbated lurking divisions. Or there are differences in cultural background or individual styles. You might even face a daunting combination of all of the above. Is there anything you can do besides keep your head down and stay out of the fray? And why should you bother?

You may not be able to turn every relationship with other teachers into a mutual admiration club, but there are important reasons to try to lighten a conflict where you can—or at least help yourself and others understand it more empathically. First, it's a drag on one's spirits to work in a place with tensions roiling just below the surface. Not good for your health, actually. Second, as you try to build connections and clarify misunderstandings, you will learn new things about yourself and the others involved. And third, you'll feel less helpless when you take actions that make your work life more sane. So finding strategies for resolving conflict contributes profoundly to your own and other teachers' power and community. As you move forward, it may help to remember the following pointers.

Big meetings aren't the place to deal with difficult topics.

One insight we gained from hard experience: *Don't* try to resolve a complex, emotionally charged difference in a big meeting unless it's guided by a highly skilled outside facilitator experienced in dealing with conflicts. Without a carefully planned structure for the discussion, people may feel the need to defend themselves vociferously and take strong stands in front of their peers. It will be hard for participants to get their story out or to listen to others, with no simple process for acknowledging and addressing each one. Feelings easily get hurt, with no ready way to repair them. You'll achieve more in small, quiet conversations where, even if strong emotions flame up, it will be easier to resolve them right away, or later if necessary.

Learn how to keep discussions constructive.

Even in private conversations, feelings can get bruised, people can feel attacked when sensitive issues are broached, or your colleague may doubt your motives. But at least in a smaller setting you can create openings to unravel the misunderstandings. Help for working through this can be found in the book *Crucial Conversations: Tools for Talking When Stakes Are High*, by Kerry Patterson and his colleagues (2002). Yes, this is a best seller, but it walks you in detail through typical heated conversations and identifies strategies that thoughtful people use to cool down and get focused on their common goals and problem solving. One technique the authors describe, for example, is to "step away" from the content—the accusations or defensive words being uttered—and, instead of answering them or defending yourself, try to identify a common purpose that you and the other person share. It's not easy in the heat of the discussion, but worth learning to do!

Find shared interests.

We learned a lot from a friend who brought a depth of experience to teaching from his first career in the corporate world. As an African American male, he's strongly committed to improving minority adolescent boys' achievement, so he organized a program to address this crucial issue in his school. He knew, however, that people hold differing beliefs about the best way to promote young minority men's success. Not surprisingly, such differences cut across racial boundaries and can be held very passionately. In this case, some teachers asserted that the program would become a crutch and undermine, rather than strengthen, the students' sense of personal efficacy.

Our friend—we'll call him John—was convinced that the program would indeed help these students by building mutual responsibility and support among them. But how could he get through to the most influential of the naysayers, a teacher who had the ear of the administration? First, John said, he "studied" his colleague, gathering information from around the school about his interests and attitudes. Next, he asked this colleague for help. He had learned that the teacher had a great interest in gathering and analyzing data. So he explained that in order to help the young men, he, John, would need as much data on them as possible. His colleague agreed and a partnership flourished. Not only was this source of opposition diverted into a constructive partnership, but the program was stronger as a result.

Focus on kids' learning.

Here's how a group of four elementary teachers at a small school worked through a racially charged misunderstanding. To promote dual language learning, they had decided that the two Latina teachers would teach science in Spanish and social studies in English. All of the students, both those with English as a first language and those with Spanish, would spend an hour a day with the Latina teachers studying these two subjects. The Latina teachers would also take an additional twenty minutes to help the English speakers with Spanish and the Spanish-speaking kids with English. But the two Anglo teachers began to feel frustrated that all this didn't leave enough time for the rest of the subjects. Their complaints were perceived as an attack on Spanish language teaching, and feelings were hurt.

After numerous attempts to clarify their concerns, the Anglo teachers realized that the real issue was *time* and kids' needs, rather than any balance between the languages. Once everyone agreed that this was a legitimate concern, the team devised a new plan with longer but less frequent periods for science and social studies. The second language work was set aside when all agreed that it wasn't proving effective. This solution wasn't ideal, they knew, and the whole school would need to rethink scheduling the following year. But the compromise plan took the pressure off, and an understanding had been achieved.

A Word About Race

It is impossible to talk about teacher power and the importance of teacher community without acknowledging the role that race in America can play in a healthy or a dysfunctional school community. Racial issues are often avoided by teachers who prefer to deny their presence or who do not know how to talk about them. Meanwhile, divisions around race can cut in all directions, often adding an additional dimension to conflicts that might otherwise be minor, complicating personal differences, bringing out people's insecurities, and making conflicts tougher to resolve. Even when racial issues sorely need to be addressed, sometimes principals, teachers, or other staff seek to gain control over or silence others instead of addressing the difficult underlying issues. Sometimes, racial concerns are reinforced when, for example, the teachers in a poor neighborhood watch a steady stream of new, underprepared white teachers arrive and then quit after a year or two, and, again, there can seem to be no way to deal with the issue. In many cases, conflicts divide blacks and whites or Latinos and African Americans; in other cases, conflicts arise within seemingly homogeneous ethnic groups, reflecting differences in social background or philosophy that are wider than some might realize.

We wish we knew all the answers to these questions, but we do believe the strategies presented in this book can help build connections between groups so they can begin to tackle the challenges and unpack the baggage of race. We know many teachers who initially saw race as an obstacle but found ways to overcome it, whether by working on relationships one-on-one or by strategically coping with specific conflicts. These teachers became more effective in their classrooms and helped build stronger multiracial communities at their schools, communities focused on students' learning, with reduced weight from society's racial baggage. In the process, they developed and made use of valuable leadership skills.

We have not found a single, neat formula for working out conflicts among school faculties, though a common theme appears to be the effort to find common ground and common purposes. Perhaps not everyone on the staff will become best friends. But these narratives help us understand how teachers who care about their professional community think and act more strategically to untangle conflicts and work constructively and respectfully with their colleagues.

In the Classroom

Building connections among various groups in the classroom and resolving conflicts depends not just on interventions in a crisis, but on the climate that you create from day one. One-on-one discussions between a teacher and individual students offer a great opportunity for climate building with students at the start of the year, establishing your interest in each student and providing important information for your work with your kids that can be helpful in settling disruptions later on. If you use a writing workshop structure, you'll be doing lots of these conferences about the kids' work anyway. But it's a good idea to focus a round at the start of the year on learning just who your students are, encouraging them to open up by sharing a few details from your own life. Two possible questions to get things started:

- Tell me about something you're interested in that I might not guess.

- What's one thing you felt good about in school last year?

Between students and teacher, the conferences will flow differently from the standard one-on-one interview. The student will be doing more of the talking, of course. Each conference might take just three to five minutes. But it's still a good idea for you to draw connections between your own life and theirs, to let students know that your own experiences help you understand what they're going through.

Address conflict constructively.

The traditional approach to settling conflicts between kids has been to assert authority: pull them apart, reprimand both, perhaps make a quick decision about who appears to have been the culprit, order one or both to apologize, and mete out some punishment. Often, however, this doesn't really settle anything. Skillful teachers, in contrast, employ various structures for more meaningfully resolving conflicts, using the events as occasions for important teaching, and making the classroom a more cohesive community where learning can proceed efficiently. Peer mediation is one well-documented approach by which trained student teams guide kids in conflict to talk through and resolve problems themselves. Regular community meetings are another. The conflict circles and related strategies developed under the label *restorative justice* offer still more options. Another valuable approach is the Responsive Classroom program (www.responsiveclassroom.org), developed by the Northeast Foundation for Children, which guides teachers to help a child involved in a disruption to really think through what took place and what a more constructive choice would look like. Kids role-play conflicts and alternative ways of responding to them. All of these approaches provide a safe, structured space in which students can work out conflicts more deeply, learn positive social behaviors, and reach understandings that repair and strengthen the classroom community.

Steve has conducted peer mediation training for many teams of students and can testify that it's a powerful learning experience and leadership training for the mediators as well as a great influence on school climate. Mediators must analyze their own language use to remain neutral and learn how to ask probing questions that bring out the details of the situation without assigning blame. These are higher-order thinking skills well worth taking the time to learn.

WHAT PRINCIPALS CAN DO

Principals we know find one-on-one interviews with teachers and students essential for building commitment to the school's mission. They are crucial for learning the true concerns, passions, and talents of the faculty and kids, and for building the basis of trust that's needed for settling conflicts constructively. Especially when new to a school and aiming to initiate new approaches, strong principals find one-on-ones exceedingly important. These conversations allow a new leader to learn what the real needs and attitudes are in a school. In a second round of individual meetings, the principal can introduce her thinking in response to what she has discovered, in a calm setting where she can explore what support or obstacles lie ahead. A series of studies by the Southwest Educational Development Laboratory on strategies used by effective principals to promote change in their schools emphasizes that "principals of outstanding schools 'listened well to parents, teachers and pupils' . . . 'developing one-to-one communication with teachers'" (Mendez-Morse 1992). Simply put, regular one-to-one talks are key to almost any change process in a school. Then when conflicts arise, the tools and strategies found in resources like *Crucial Conversations* (Patterson et al. 2002) will help the principal work on them in the same ways as we've described for teachers. And the principal will be modeling constructive problem solving as well.

Take Action
in the
Building

Go Meta

6

How It Helps You

Teaching is not an assembly-line job, though sometimes we may feel like it is when hordes of students pass before us every day. It's a profession, built on deep philosophical, theoretical, and historical foundations, even if we don't always think about them. So to hone our craft and come to a larger understanding of our work—which is a prerequisite for teacher leadership and teacher power—we need time beyond the classroom. Time for planning together and making thoughtful decisions about curriculum, instruction, and school climate. Time to chew over a problem by talking with a trusted colleague. And alone time to reflect on individual kids, on classroom strategies that rocked or bombed, on approaches that are new to us, and on what we are learning about larger issues that affect our work.

whole school partner individual

We can bear down more and more, trying to make some strategy work with our kids, and end up burning out. Or we can step back, analyze what's happening, and look for a fresh approach, working smarter rather than harder. Yes, other professionals also feel overworked and deprived of time for planning and reflection. But teachers—especially the best teachers, because we're trying to do so much—are particularly crunched for quality thinking time and need more of it to reflect, both with colleagues and on our own.

Make It Work:
Reflect and Plan Together

Innovative schools find a lot more time than others for faculty to plan and share thoughts and ideas. Telpochcalli School and Namaste Charter School, both in Chicago, release students after lunch every Friday afternoon for teachers to work either as a whole staff, in teams, or individually. Namaste teachers rotate the Fridays—one for whole-staff professional development, the next for grade-level meetings, the third for vertical teams, and finally one for individual work. Schools like Al Raby, McAuliffe School, and Whittier School, also in Chicago, use online discussion groups to keep communication going beyond meeting times.

Carlene Murphy (1997), for Focus on Results, catalogued ways that schools set aside time for teachers. Some of the more creative approaches:

- bring in four or five substitutes once a month and rotate them from one class to another for one-hour stretches, so that five or six groups of five teachers each can meet in study groups over the course of the day

- pair teachers to cover their own plus their partner's class together for an hour, so as to release faculty groups for professional book study sessions (The combined classes consist of reading or writing workshop, clubs, or other flexible activities.)

- replace alternate weekly faculty meetings with study group sessions

If you teach at a school where creative scheduling has not been the rule, there are several strategies for creating common reflection and development time. One option is to carve it out yourself with a small like-minded group—a lunchtime book-discussion group, an independent study graduate course arranged through a supportive university faculty member, or a research project among several teachers to look at student work or to figure out how to respond to particular classroom challenges (see Chapter 3). Another approach is to advocate for more common planning time in your school or district. That's what Janine Givens-Belsley did successfully at her school; you can learn more about her story in Chapter 9.

Time!

We don't know a single teacher alive who doesn't agonize, with complete justification, about the lack of time for reflection, serious talk with colleagues, collaborative planning, finding more resources for her classroom, and reaching out beyond the school. It's a rare school that allows sufficient common planning or staff development time, and sometimes when it *is* provided, the activity isn't well planned (to put it politely). And for a whole school trying to institute a serious distributed leadership structure, the lack of common work time is even more severe.

Getting Over It

OK, this is not an obstacle we can just get over. Unlike many professions, and unlike education systems in many other countries, most American schools don't budget much time for collaboration.

Nevertheless, when a common activity is valuable enough, teachers simply make time, in spite of all the obstacles. At Huntsville School, in Huntsville, Ohio, for example, teachers have treasured the Wednesday mornings before school when they gather to discuss a professional article or book chapter and talk about their work, and they've sworn to continue it permanently, no matter who is principal or what new program is introduced. This developed out of their ongoing work on literacy with education consultant Regie Routman (Zemelman and Daniels 2005, 288–91). As this history suggests, building a meaningful context first can make all the difference in a faculty's resolve to make time for reflection and use it well.

Make it worth the time.

So there's precious little time set aside for planning and reflection. And what's more the time that is available is not always used to greatest advantage. A recent study by the Consortium on Chicago School Research (Stevens 2006) that we mentioned in Chapter 4 showed that even in small schools where teachers are more supportive of one another and enjoy a positive professional climate, most of the talk is not about teaching and learning, but limited to everyday problem solving. So just as important as finding time for reflection is what teachers do with it. Here are some ideas from successful schools.

birdwalks

Plan interdisciplinary learning projects together. When Best Practice High School, in Chicago, was at the height of its success, teachers at each grade level planned and conducted interdisciplinary study projects several times each year. These not only were fascinating and engaging projects for the students but also provided a setting for teachers to debate and apply ideas about good teaching together (Daniels, Bizar, and Zemelman 2001). During meeting time, the teachers talked a great deal about approaches and philosophies, but they also had to reach agreement and prepare to execute a plan.

Review research and target an important problem. In other schools (such as those working with the Targeted Leadership Consulting organization), an instructional leadership team reviews data, research, and information from experts in order to identify and address an important need or problem at the school. The team then guides the school to implement new strategies to address the needs that have been identified.

Form a Critical Friends Group. A very effective structure for reflection widely used by the Coalition of Essential Schools is the Critical Friends Group. While the name may sound a little daunting, the processes are fascinating and constructive. This strategy brings together a small group of teachers to discuss in a structured way a problem or challenge facing one member or perhaps the whole group. Well-designed protocols guide the group (available in the *National School Reform Faculty Resource Book*, published by the National School Reform Faculty [2007–8], and on the organization's website) and provide excellent tools for facilitating discussion. Each protocol structures the talk in a unique way, focusing participants as they share ideas, listen, reflect, and respond.

So how does a discussion protocol work? Two examples follow:

- "Back to the Future" (developed by Scott Murphy, in the *National School Reform Faculty Resource Book*, 23–24) focuses on a plan or project that a teacher or team intends to execute. After someone presents the plan, the group asks clarifying questions and receives responses. These are followed by "probing questions," to get everyone thinking more deeply. The presenter can respond or just quietly listen as these questions are posed. The group then pretends the plan has already been implemented and imagines what success will look like. Next, the group "looks back," envisioning the project's start and the steps to get it done. Again, the presenter just listens. Finally, the presenter and group together discuss whether any steps need to be added to ensure success. The presenter shares thoughts about what she has gained from the discussion, and the whole group reflects on how the process worked. This protocol enables a group to analyze and evaluate a project as objectively as possible, removing the ego involvement so common to even the most productive meetings.

● "Issaqua" (developed by Nancy Mohr, Deborah Bambino, and Daniel Baron, in the *National School Reform Faculty Resource Book*, 26–27) is a more challenging protocol, but when Steve observed a group of teachers using it to help a first-year colleague with classroom discipline, the teachers were comfortable and trusting. In one step, group members restate in "active listening" mode the problem that has been presented, and in the next, they offer "interpretive" comments (not advice) to reflect on how they understand the issues raised. These aren't necessarily intuitive ways of talking through a problem. The discussion in this case was led by a trained teacher facilitator. It allowed the presenting teacher to receive thoughtful ideas from peers in a well-organized, nonjudgmental way, for which she was extremely grateful.

Make time for your own reflection.

Whether your school is as innovative as the one where Steve observed that Issaqua protocol or a place where, as with many schools, such practices are in scarce supply, you need to create a space in which you can reflect productively on your own. Following are some ways teachers we know have done this.

Get to school early. Social studies and GIS teacher Sarah Giddings, at Al Raby High School for Community and Environment, is a morning person. "I get to school very early. Things are quiet between seven and eight, and I'm by myself to get my classroom setup ready and out of the way. This leaves me time for networking during the day. We also use lots of email and a Google Groups account to keep up lots of ongoing communication among our staff."

Attend a professional conference every year. Lori Birenberg, also at Al Raby, makes sure she gets to one or two professional conferences every year. She likes small local events, preferrably ones that are teacher led. And she doesn't listen passively. "If it doesn't get me thinking about my own classroom, then it's not worth it."

So what about students' loss of quality learning time while she's gone? Her answer: "I'm a control freak because it's typically unproductive when a substitute is called in, so it's really hard for me to be away from the kids. But it's probably good for them. Sometimes they need a break from me, and I need a break from them. Too many teachers feel like the kids can't manage without them. But I think that's a dangerous attitude, and not a good way to approach teaching. It means you think your way is the only way for them to learn." We would add that we've seen some teachers build routines, student roles, and classroom responsibilities so that kids continue working whether their regular teacher is present or not.

Keep a journal. Last winter, Al Raby science teacher Evan Roberts took the plunge. Over the nine months between starting his journal and the date of our discussion, he averaged about one entry per week, usually drafted late at night. As an African American male high school science teacher, Evan is passionate about the struggles, marginalization, and misperceptions that continue to make life difficult for his students. Unlike the personal ramblings some include in their journals, Evan's entries are almost like editorials or short essays. He writes about sexism, about the negative messages teenagers hear every day, the trivialized portrayals of iconic black leaders of the past, and the books and speeches by outstanding black scholars that have inspired him. For example, thinking about Black History Month, Evan writes,

> Thinking back to my childhood days, I can vividly remember the school celebrations for Black history month. I remember learning about Harriet Tubman's Underground Railroad, Charles Drew's work with blood plasma, reciting Martin Luther King's "I Have a Dream" speech. . . . Unfortunately, I saw in my students what I personally experienced as a student who had been through years of similar Black history celebrations. The students were not as excited as I hoped they would be. In fact, it seemed as though they were listless. I felt that the foundation of their listlessness may have rested on the idea that these heroes and heroines had been acknowledged long before, and therefore what was the point of going through what they did and how they did it? . . . The fundamental problem that we face today is that many people celebrate Black history not realizing that they do so through "white lenses" or from a European perspective. Celebrating Black/African history this way creates a serious problem because it limits our achievements as only a response to the savage institution of slavery, and not to the inherent greatness of a flourishing culture Africans independently established.

How does this journal writing help Evan Roberts with his teaching? He said that it has led him to rethink assignments, jettison busywork, and ask himself at every turn, "Why am I asking students to do this?" Evan reads extensively to further this thinking—books, for example, by Asa Hilliard, Lisa Delpit,

Martin Haberman, and Gloria Ladson-Billings. As Ladson-Billings herself has observed, "teachers are [i.e., need to be] cognizant of themselves as political beings" (1994, 118). You can't be a great teacher without developing this kind of wider perspective.

Tina Boyer-Brown, another avid journal keeper, sits down with her morning coffee before school and writes several pages each day on her teaching, venting, or "getting [her] head together." She told us she often falls asleep thinking about something she'll write about the next morning. She started this practice a year before she began teaching, inspired by Julia Cameron's widely acclaimed book *The Artist's Way: A Spiritual Path to Higher Creativity* (2002). The journaling process, she testified, has been the biggest tool for growth that she has found, helping with major life decisions including the one that took her from the corporate world to her teaching career.

In the Classroom

In Chapter 2 we described how teachers at Namaste Charter School realized through shadowing students that they needed to help kids become more aware of their learning by making learning goals clear, rather than just marching mindlessly through their lessons. Students and teachers both need time to reflect on their work—to remember, to value, to realize what worked and what didn't, and to consider how they'll do it differently next time. When Maia Golley helps her first graders develop habits of reflection in writing workshop, it doesn't just come up at the end of a task but requires plenty of preparation and focus. Up front, she makes clear what she's going to show them in the minilessons she presents: "Today, I want to explain to you how to add good details so the reader can really picture what you are talking about." And then she reminds the kids as she models the strategy: "OK, so I just showed you how to. . . . " Next, in individual conferences, she'll ask, "Remember when we were talking about adding details today?" and talk with the student about how he has used this strategy. Finally, she asks students to explain orally why they've chosen particular pieces to share, and then they begin to exercise reflection on their own, drawing on their increasing awareness of the strategies Maia is teaching. Of course, Maia explained, it takes a couple of weeks and lots of repetition for their awareness of each strategy to sink in. "You have to be patient," she observed. "Kids don't usually understand how to reflect without being taught."

Staff meetings must inevitably address immediate needs—scheduling changes, paperwork due, special events to be arranged, security issues, and more. But a thoughtful leader can start meetings with ten minutes of reflection. Allocate five minutes for teachers to jot on a card, "One thing I've been thinking about in our school or with our kids is . . . ," and then five minutes more for several teachers to share their responses either with the whole group or in pairs. And if these comment cards become too gripey, urge, "If you have a complaint, offer one practical suggestion to help address it." Some school leaders have a suggestion box, but a more active approach signals that reflection is important. Some principals write their own reflection letters periodically, to model the practice and encourage important conversations.

Time is of course the great challenge to achieving more reflection among teachers, and its allocation is often determined by conditions that appear beyond our control. On the other hand, Linda Darling-Hammond studied a number of schools that were successful at finding more common planning time for teachers. It takes creativity and a belief in the effectiveness of this kind of time. At one Boston school, the principal designed several innovative arrangements. One was to work with a local university to place advanced student teachers in the school as paraprofessionals, so that if the teacher was out of the room, the kids were working with a qualified adult. Another was to have outside teachers who ran after-school programs overlap in the classrooms for the last hour of the day, freeing up regular staff. Obviously these arrangements required negotiation, respectively, with the district, the partner university, or the after-school provider organization. But they accomplished the planning-time goal and also deepened the involvement of partners with the school (Miles and Darling-Hammond 1997).

For many of us, the Web has helped with the time problem by enabling teacher conversations to unfold without everyone being in the same room at the same time. We would caution, however, that a tool is only as good as the practices of the people who use it. We know of online conversation sites that have fallen into disuse or become mere bulletin boards for bureaucratic announcements or day-to-day practical concerns. A good school leader can ensure this doesn't happen by sharing thoughts and reflections on the site himself and by using the site to initiate conversations across the school.

Speak Up

7

How It Helps You

When teachers think about whether or not to speak up at a faculty meeting, many picture a choice between two extremes. Either you'll challenge the school leadership or you'll lie low so as not to cause trouble, get in trouble, or be seen as trouble by your fellow teachers. But to be fully developed in your career, you need to be an active contributor to a professional community, which means finding a productive third path—a way to speak out that is strategic and accomplishes something worthwhile.

Why is it important to find your voice? Well, for one, it gives you the opportunity to state your needs and get them met. If you never speak up, decisions will be made by others—others who don't fully understand how these decisions will affect you. When you voice your thoughts, things may not always go your way, but instead of just griping about problems in the teachers' lounge, you will know you tried your best. As you develop skills to speak up reasonably, constructively, and strategically, you will be helping to make your school a more professional and thoughtful place.

Maia Golley at Namaste Charter School learned a lesson about beginning strategically soon after her arrival: "I realized I would have to push myself. The school was relatively new, but was up and running before I started there. So I had to figure out what was going on before I could contribute. At one meeting on co-teaching, I wondered out loud if the effort would need more of a structure. This was not a popular idea, and that took the wind out of my sails. I realized that it would be a good idea to check in with a few people first before bringing something up in a larger arena."

Make It Work: Practical Steps for Speaking Up Constructively

At so many of the meetings we have attended, even when a teacher or two took the risk of standing up to give a passionate speech and stir things up, there was no follow-through, so any potential changes were stillborn. A little thoughtful strategizing will help ensure that the ideas you voice will lead to productive action.

What are a few key principles to consider as you prepare to say your piece? We posed this question to our colleague Kim Zalent, who as a community organizer trained by the Industrial Areas Foundation has provided guidance for teachers and leaders in a number of innovative and successful schools in Chicago and New York. Kim helped us devise the following suggestions.

Decide on the risk level.

If the topic is controversial, it's understandable that many teachers may ask themselves, "Do I need to worry about my job if I say something?" In some schools, the leader will have established a sense of safety for addressing hard issues. In others the atmosphere may be intimidating. Your own personality also comes into play. Perhaps you are simply shy. Alternatively, you may be like high school teacher Janine Givens-Belsley, who explained, "I can't stand to be in a situation where I have something to say and not say it." The people we know who decided to speak up even when they thought it risky actually ended up being respected by the administration and even promoted! There's a balance in here somewhere: you don't want to become a constant annoyance, but you limit your professional life if you never take any risks at all.

Be clear about what you want to accomplish.

How much have you already worked on your plan, and what action do you want to come out of the discussion you initiate? It's one thing to float a new idea and another to bring out a fully developed proposal. Will it be a good idea for a committee to flesh out a plan? Try a pilot version first? Gather some data

It's Too Political

We often think that speaking up or taking action outside our classrooms will be seen as challenging those in charge—risky; or it seems political, with messy maneuvering or compromises we don't really believe in. In plenty of schools, making too many suggestions, or disagreeing with the principal, or proposing to change a policy is seen as challenging authority.

Getting Over It

The traditional view that equates leadership with bossing others around and being political is one of the many unfortunate myths that make us want to redefine what real leadership means. We need to understand that speaking up and seeking ways to support one another are crucial acts that contribute to positive change. They don't need to challenge anybody. They simply start the work of improving the school or some portion of it. Karen Sabaka has taught kindergarten and first grade for seven years at Telpochcalli School in Chicago, a small school focused on art and dual language education. Karen described how she began taking an active part in the teacher community early in her career:

> When I started teaching, I didn't have a clear idea of what I was supposed to be doing. So I looked for resources—books to read, workshops to go to. I asked the other teachers in my cluster, "What's our plan for literacy?" We didn't have one. I had attended a workshop I liked, and I suggested that the leader come to do a summer workshop, just for our cluster, so we could start creating a plan. I wanted to improve my own practice, and I figured other people would want that, too.

in the school to clarify the need for the project? Whatever you decide, griping by itself produces little change, so what's a constructive, practical step you can propose?

Talk with the principal first.

Leaders and administrators do not like surprises. And by checking in with them first, you may be able to win crucial support right up front—or realize issues that must be addressed in order to get the idea accepted. When Janine Givens-Belsley decided to lobby for planning time at a school where she taught, she made sure the principal knew she was working on it before consulting with other teachers (see Chapter 9, "Mount a Campaign," page 94). To prepare for this conversation, think about how you will bring up your proposal. Tentative inquiry works well: "I was wondering if you have been concerned about. . . . " And then, "What do you think about this as a solution?" When Janine first approached her principal, he was vaguely noncommittal, but that provided enough room to move ahead. Even if the principal is opposed to your idea at first, at least you know where things stand and can consider strategically how best to proceed.

Lay the groundwork by building on your relationships with fellow teachers.

Maia Golley's realization after her first, embarrassing effort was a good one. Talking with key faculty members will not only build support for your idea but put you in touch with other perspectives, questions, and concerns you may need to consider. Of course, it's helpful to have established good relationships with these people before you even start talking (see Chapter 4, "Open the Classroom Door," page 47, and Chapter 5, "Build Bridges," page 56). When Ignacio Lopez wanted his high school in Chicago to initiate a school newsletter for parents, he first shared the idea with his English department to get his colleagues' reactions. He reported, "[Then] I went to a writing center teacher to get this parent newsletter accepted, and she helped me revise a few things, so I felt really confident selling this thing to the staff." In another example, when Steve and his school-reform partner Kim Zalent were launching the Chicago Schools Alliance, a network of Chicago schools, they met with each of the participating principals. One school leader explained that when people previously tried to establish such a group, it had floundered because they'd gotten tangled in an endless debate about qualifications for joining. This provided a great heads-up about how *not* to get started.

Decide whether speaking out at a meeting is the best strategy.

Are you dealing with one of the many little issues that harass teachers every day or something much bigger? When Harry was teaching high school, there were never enough tables in the rooms, but he found that making friends with the engineer early in the morning got him the desired tables more effectively than complaining at a meeting. And if the issue is at all sensitive, discussing it in a large meeting may be the least productive option. Misunderstandings can spiral out of control and damage your cause. In sensitive cases, quiet one-on-one talks with a series of colleagues may be the best strategy. A teacher at one school where the faculty is very committed to social justice described the hurt feelings that emerged from the occasional faculty "town hall meetings" on controversies relating to race. "They're always a failure," she said. As an alternative, she and fellow teachers organized small-group book discussions on texts such as *Other People's Children*, by Lisa Delpit (1995), and *Waging Peace in Our Schools*, by Linda Lantieri and Janet Patti (1996). These discussions, she found, were much more positive and productive.

Especially if the issue is sensitive, plan thoroughly.

OK, so you've decided to try to initiate a full-faculty discussion. How will you respond to the hard questions? What compromises are you prepared to make? Who will speak up to support you? (Developing a floor team can ensure that you aren't sticking your neck out alone.) How will you word statements to keep the tone positive?

Stay focused on your goal and don't get drawn into unproductive fights.

All too often, faculty discussions and professional disagreements turn personal. If someone is opposed to your idea and tries to head the talk in this direction, don't take the bait. Instead, continue calmly to explain your idea and seek action on it. This can be hard to do, but it's worth the inner effort. Often, the trouble comes from just one or two curmudgeons who have learned to manipulate the group and sidetrack new ideas, and they retreat when they see they are isolated. Our friend Ignacio Lopez refers to these resistors as *ducks* or *quackers*, because whenever anybody suggests a constructive project, they start quacking about all of the difficulties of implementing it. As we've suggested in other chapters, it may help to have one-on-one discussions with such people in advance, to open a real dialogue with them. But if that doesn't work, don't let them turn your explanation into a personal tug-of-war or pull you away from your objective.

▓ In the Classroom

Naturally, our students need to learn how to speak up confidently, too, and develop their own leadership skills. Group participation is not necessarily a skill children develop on their own. But this is a little easier to tackle than our own reticence, since as teachers we can implement specific strategies to make the setting safe and have ideas received respectfully by both the teacher and the rest of the kids. Following are some strategies to start creating an atmosphere of safety and mutual respect in your classroom.

Guide your class to make some positive rules and stick to them.

Good teachers help students create a set of rules for respectful listening and responding. These go up on chart paper, but be sure to remind kids regularly about them and hold class meetings to reflect on breakdowns. In some classes we visit, the rules get made but soon become just part of the classroom wallpaper.

Role-play various scenarios so students can compare positive (and negative) behaviors for speaking out.

Many children need help learning to ask in a constructive way for what they need, instead of just demanding or acting out. Teachers who use the Responsive Classroom program find role-playing especially effective with young children, though older kids and adults enjoy it as well. In fact, much of Responsive Classroom is designed to give students voice in a structured manner (www .responsiveclassroom.org).

Start a classroom writing workshop.

The writing workshop structure, a favorite for teaching composition and using writing as a learning tool in content areas, includes a sharing session at the end of each workshop period. Students learn to give constructive feedback and ask helpful questions through teacher modeling and repeated practice. We once observed a second-grade boy read his basketball story during writing workshop, and it consisted only of baskets and scores. Children patiently asked about the event until he looked down and commented, "I think I need to revise this." The teacher had taught the kids to ask their probing questions respectfully and let the writer determine how to address them. So the kids were able to continue sharing their work without fear of being put down.

Use explicit strategies to help students find their voices.

Especially when first learning these skills, students often need more time than we realize to organize their thoughts and frame responses to you and each other. Good teachers in all subject areas often employ brief stop-and-write moments—just a minute or two in the middle or at the end of an activity when students jot a response to a question or idea, or ask a question themselves. These stop-and-writes broaden the range of participation, ensuring that two or three outgoing students do not do all of the talking. Some good teachers we know also require the class to take notes on student presentations and use them to ask questions of the presenters.

WHAT PRINCIPALS CAN DO

Guiding a whole faculty to speak up and listen to one another can be a complex effort. Just as in the classroom, adults in a school need shared ground rules for respectful interaction and explicit strategies to encourage them to contribute their professional opinions. Teachers will watch to see what points of view the principal supports and gauge whether it's safe to speak their minds, so signaling openness to differences is essential. Perhaps most discouraging for discussion are the long lists of announcements, everyday procedures, and declarations of the latest rules and policies.

One practical step is to *include a substantive educational item in every meeting*. Start the meeting with this. Whether meetings occur before or after school, the tail end is not the time for deep discussion. In the early morning, teachers will be thinking about getting ready for the kids. After school, the day's weariness will only grow deeper as the minutes tick by. So invite a different teacher to introduce the topic at the beginning of each meeting, ensuring that the session begins with a faculty voice. At the end of the meeting, teachers can list on exit slips the important topics we didn't get to this time.

Meanwhile, signals of openness must go far beyond the meetings. When teachers come forward with a new idea, they need encouragement. While schools can't tackle more than a few big efforts at once, the school can prioritize these plans thoughtfully together, rather than by fiat.

At bottom, this is about *building trust*. Anthony Bryk and Barbara Schneider, in *Trust in Schools: A Core Resource for Improvement* (2002), explain that "relational trust" involves reducing people's sense of risk through mutual respect, belief in each other's competence, a significant level of personal regard, and a sense of people's integrity. The studies that Bryk guided at the Consortium for Chicago School Research bear out that student achievement improved more in schools where higher levels of such trust were present.

So what are some ways to work toward establishing this kind of trust?

- *Be positive.* Teachers look to the principal to model the school's acceptable behaviors; being critical encourages venting and griping. Conversely, when a principal is positive and constructive, even when she doesn't agree with everything a teacher is suggesting, teachers will follow her lead.

- *Listen.* In a paper from the Southwest Educational Development Laboratory, Sylvia Mendez-Morse (1992) surveyed the many research studies highlighting principals' need for effective listening and communicating. This means more than an open-door policy. At McAuliffe School in Chicago, the assistant principal was delighted with teachers' appreciation for the one-on-one talks she arranged after we introduced the idea.

- *Learn.* Over the years, we've again and again heard teachers appreciate administrators who understand the challenges they deal with and scorn those who know little about their work but try to hide behind arbitrary mandates. So no matter how many years a principal has spent in the classroom, it's important to continue to be a learner. She can find interesting articles on teaching and share these with the faculty. At one highly successful school, teachers often remarked on how much they appreciated this sharing.

- *From the start, be clear with yourself and your faculty on the extent to which teachers will be participating in decision making.* At one school, the administrators worked to promote "teacher voice" in order to win faculty support for a change they wanted. Later on, however, when a decision was made without consultation, teachers reacted, "You want our support when you need us to get something accomplished, but now that you don't need us, you're not interested in what we have to say. So much for teacher voice." Clearly, it would have helped for the school leader to have decided up front and explicitly communicated which issues were open for discussion.

Deal with Committees 8

How It Helps You

It is easy to be cynical about committees and meetings. At too many schools, they go nowhere or their reports just end up in a file cabinet. But it is impossible to achieve substantial school changes without them. The problem is most people haven't been trained in how to set them up, run them, and disband them when they're no longer needed. These skills are rarely taught because they're considered second nature, which is far from true, as most of us learn the hard way. But when a committee is formed with a clear and realizable purpose, when everyone comes to agree on its aims, when people grow accustomed to coming to meetings prepared, and when someone takes responsibility for planning them, running them, and distributing the minutes and other results in writing, immeasurable frustration can be avoided. When committees and teams function efficiently, they can make everyone's teaching—and schools—much more productive and rewarding. This kind of outcome is especially needed in a place where time is extremely limited and people are stretched to maximum capacity.

Education schools and even new-teacher mentoring programs rarely teach how to manage meetings and projects, perhaps because teaching has for so long been seen as a solo career in which working on teams or committees is considered just an add-on. We've talked with many teachers who said that soon after they began teaching, they were asked to run a committee or a meeting but felt unready, so they had to figure out on the job what worked.

Of course, teachers have always needed to collaborate with others in their building to plan and grade together and to work on projects they cared about. It's not difficult to work with friends on issues close to your heart and your classroom. Teachers have also worked together more formally in high school departments and in elementary and middle school teams, and while our recommendations about meetings apply to these groups, the strategies we discuss here are meant to go beyond these formal units. It is becoming increasingly necessary to work with teachers and staff you don't know that well—or even colleagues with whom you have issues—on projects that benefit not only your classroom but the whole school (see Chapter 5, "Build Bridges"). Three typical tasks for such committees follow:

- *Addressing the whole child.* In recognizing that the whole school needs to address the whole child, committees with representatives from all segments of the faculty need to be able to work together. Sure, some doubters who do not see the need to collaborate will require a little nudging. But if the process is done right, they will actually enjoy adapting and become better teachers. It is hard to overstate the support that having a whole building behind you will provide for your teaching and your kids as you work your heart out to educate all of them.

- *Coordinating curriculum and instruction.* It really makes no sense to talk about an excellent curriculum for one class or grade without knowing how it fits into students' graduation outcomes. Curriculum committees and cross-disciplinary teams can ensure that the school is covering learning needs in a thoughtful sequence, avoiding unnecessary repetition, and addressing gaps in learning. Teacher collaboration is just as essential to instruction. It is worth addressing the ways various teaching styles support one another—or leave students confused—if faculty members are to understand how each contributes to the success of the whole. Committees can analyze student work to see what additional efforts the school may need in order to meet its goals. And let's not forget how committees can help address students' needs beyond the classroom, whether to strengthen advisories or implement other schoolwide strategies for keeping kids on track. We all know how much easier it is to work at a school in which everybody has the whole child at heart and we don't lose kids in all of the compartmentalization.

- *Taking on additional whole-school issues.* In many schools, faculty teams take responsibility for the new-teacher induction process. Committees can provide a unified face to parents, board and community members, and other partners—thinking through policies rather than just responding to crises. Strategic planning for the whole school is also much more effective when teachers are involved. At some schools we know, faculty and staff also sit on hiring committees as well as committees on policy changes, for example, in teacher schedules. And some teacher teams that work best are just devoted to collaborative reading of new articles or books, a refreshing retreat from the hectic life of the classroom.

With all of this work to be done, even if you don't feel comfortable heading up a committee right away, it is a smart idea to volunteer for one. Not only can you learn from a less pressured vantage point what to do or not do, but you can learn a great deal about your school, your colleagues, and your district that you can rarely figure out just from talking to friends. Without seeming like someone who needs to take over, you can play a part in making decisions that have a major impact on your teaching. A number of teachers, for example, have described how sitting on the technology committee meant they were the first ones to have access to newer technology and training—not a bad perk in exchange for a little of your time.

Make It Work

So you are asked to be on a committee, or you volunteer to sit on or even facilitate one. What can you do to make this a fulfilling rather than an onerous task? If you have some control or influence, how can you make group meetings effective? Following are nine suggestions.

Clarify the purpose.

The tendency is to start a group—whether a grade team, a school-improvement plan team, a curriculum committee, or even a department—and then hold meetings because you're a group and that's what groups do. Actually, the most productive meetings are often ad hoc; maybe it's not even a real committee, but just four or five people reading together or working on a task they or the principal want done. And even if this is a standing committee, it's worth questioning whether a particular meeting needs to occur and what the goals should be. A meeting functions best with a limited number of objectives, agreed upon beforehand. Once an ad hoc committee has fulfilled its purpose, it is time to disband. Even "permanent" committees can include sunset provisions so they expire automatically at the end of the year unless enough people see a need to continue. This prevents burnout from overcommitment and meeting just to meet.

Build *commitment.*

While you may not always be able to control membership, the point is to bring in people who are excited about the project and willing to take on their share of the work. It's better to have a smaller committee than to have members who don't show up regularly, are just marking time, or are not completing their contributions.

Find *the right time.*

The best time is a joint prep or lunch period, but some faculties prefer after school. Mornings before school are not optimal because most of us are planning the day ahead, and some of us are bleary-eyed and not ready to focus.

OK, teacher power sounds great! But I'm no good at running a committee or getting a proposal accepted by my administration!

Exactly. Most of us have never been explicitly taught how to get things done in an organization, how to reach out, build bridges, cross factional lines, work together on a project, or deal with professional conflicts. Even the widely acclaimed National Board Certification process does not ask about these skills.

Getting Over It

Well, we're teachers. We believe in education, for kids and for ourselves. We can learn these skills, as Karen Sabaka at Telpochcalli School found she needed to:

> I like to just do something and get it done. So when I started leading a committee at school I had to learn to slow down. Even though it took longer, I had to learn to let everyone talk it over and give their opinion about how things should be done.

As we said in our introduction, leadership is not about who you are or some inherent personality trait. It's about things you can do, and you already do a number of them. So now is a good time to start learning more.

Prepare well beforehand.

Meetings are more productive when the participants read materials first and come prepared with ideas and questions. Circulate a sheet in advance with a limited number of goals, an agenda, preferably with times allotted, and notes. If you are going to analyze student evidence, it's sometimes helpful to include the students' work. If the group will be reviewing a rough draft of a document, provide that, too (though if it's on a sensitive issue, talk to people first so they don't arrive ready to fight). A draft encourages everybody to focus on the task and to realize a product will emerge, not just talk. Even distributing a draft list of questions can help participants get down to business faster.

Designate roles.

Yes, all participants on the committee should have defined jobs, rotated to give everybody ownership. In addition to a facilitator, a secretary and a timekeeper are essential. (It's always easier when someone other than the facilitator enforces the rules, so the leader can avoid the appearance of bullying.) Others can prepare and present materials, summarize major decisions, or write on the board. Everybody should have tasks for follow-up work as well. Fifth-grade teacher Juli Ross is quiet by nature and never imagined herself in a leadership position, but defined roles helped her get started: "One thing we did in breeding leadership: we took turns with roles—timekeeper, agenda setter, recorder, facilitator—in team meetings. This is how I got started. Everybody has to have a responsibility. Otherwise everyone's just sitting there—especially if you're hesitant, you never have a chance to share—but this way everybody has something to contribute, something to do."

Structure the process.

To have everyone just show up and start talking is an invitation to chaos. The structure depends a lot on the size of the group, but it could be argued that four or five is the maximum number of people who can work productively on a task. Larger groups will probably need to break into subgroups to get the work done. Participants should have a basic knowledge of Robert's Rules of Order, easily gained from the short summary on the official Robert's Rules website (www.robertsrules.com). Everybody should have a sense of the time needed to reach the meeting goals, and it is usually a good idea to follow these time limits, unless a majority votes to extend an important activity or discussion. It is helpful for somebody to write the key points on the board or project them on a screen and for the facilitator to reiterate and clarify each decision briefly before the group moves on to the next agenda item.

No matter what the goals of the meeting are, it's a good idea to start with five to ten minutes for team building and bonding. Everybody can share a personal reflection, perhaps about the meeting or topic, the day, or the school year. This will help participants let go of their outside worries and prepare to focus on the task at hand.

Use technology.

Computers make it easy to keep minutes and notes in real time without having to go back and type them up. You can edit documents as a group on a big screen or at a desk and project visual aids to support the work. PowerPoint presentations and Excel spreadsheets and their Mac equivalents are also great for documenting findings. Even more helpful are Web discussion groups, including free ones like Google Groups, PBWiki, and Nicenet, and those that cost a little money but sometimes set up free hubs for schools. Some of these sites are built specifically to manage long-term projects, making it easy to organize messages by thematic threads, email the whole group or subgroups, keep track of benchmarks with built-in calendars, and post information in many different formats.

Agree on norms.

The group should set some expectations for how discussions will proceed. First the basics: The facilitator or timekeeper can make sure that everybody has a chance to speak before anybody speaks twice. Participants should think in terms of solutions and not just problems, and complaining should be avoided. No interrupting others, speaking for a long time, or digressing. It is very helpful for participants to learn strategies for holding constructive conversations about difficult issues. Two good sources for this are *Crucial Conversations* (Patterson et al. 2002) and the *National School Reform Faculty Resource Book* (National School Reform Faculty 2007–8; available from www.nsrfharmony.org). The latter includes many useful meeting and conversation protocols. These books recommend that participants stick to *I* statements and avoid evaluating other speakers' opinions.

The *National School Reform Faculty Resource Book* helps distinguish between "probing" and "clarifying" questions—both of which are more constructive than "suggestions" (54–55):

Examples of Suggestions (Avoid)

- How about trying this activity in a different grouping?

- This might work better if you allowed more time for the students to complete the project.

Examples of Clarifying Questions (Good)

- How were the students grouped?

- How long did the activity take?

Examples of Probing Questions (Also Good)

- What do you think would have happened if the students were grouped differently?

- What would the students involved define as quality work?

While the aim is to reach consensus, it is usually not productive to spend too much time trying to win over every participant, so a vote sometimes helps settle a controversy. At the same time, nobody should feel pressured to go along with the majority.

Follow up with action.

Unfortunately, many exciting initiatives in schools lose steam almost immediately. A productive meeting ends, participants return to their many responsibilities, and three weeks later they wonder what happened to all the great energy. So it's crucial to conclude with a detailed action plan. Who will oversee the project, who will be doing what task and by when, what will happen if it doesn't get done, and when's the next meeting? Even more casual meetings—a book discussion, for example—can benefit from a write-up documenting the topic and some important points. Minutes need not be formal but should be sent out quickly, especially when they contain information participants need for their tasks. If the group studied student work, include brief analyses of findings, perhaps in chart or graph form, along with actions you planned—new assignments, cross-disciplinary rubrics, or steps to include more teachers. In any ongoing project, every participant should have homework to be completed by the next meeting for all to review. If the goal is to review a policy and present recommendations to a larger faculty group or the administration or board, the result might be a one-page white paper.

Lori Birenberg stressed the importance of follow-up at her small urban high school. "On one committee at Al Raby, the group talked extensively about standardized test prep efforts for the kids but never put their ideas down." When no productive action follows a meeting because there's no written plan to follow, people will conclude, accurately, that the meeting was a waste of time. So Lori obtained an action plan sheet and edited it to fit her needs. Now she uses a "project management" approach, helping her committee decide on one project to address and see to completion over the course of a full school year.

While it helps to read up on organizing meetings and managing projects, nothing beats real-life experience. Sarah Giddings works on the student development committee at her high school because she's passionate about it and feels she has something to offer. She explained, "When you are leading a committee, you need to know where each member's strength lies and work to that strength. . . . You also need patience. Other people's time lines may differ from yours. You can set a deadline for work to be completed, but people need reminders because we're all so busy." In one case, a teacher was slow sharing the resources she had amassed. To get her to send them out for a Wednesday deadline, Sarah needed to send email reminders Monday and Tuesday and drop by the teacher's room Thursday when they hadn't arrived. Lo and behold, on Friday they at last appeared in people's in-boxes.

No matter how foreign this kind of committee work might feel at first, you'll be gratified when the results enable you to achieve real improvements—and when collaboration with your colleagues makes teaching more fun. Juli Ross explained, "I figured out that you have to be on the search committee. We'd been too late in starting searches. We didn't have viable candidates. I started selfishly [joining because my friends were on them], then started liking being on those committees." Juli ended up becoming the faculty chair of her school and did an outstanding job keeping collaborative momentum going, even though she often admitted that she couldn't believe that she had agreed to take the job. If Juli can do it, so can you.

In the Classroom

In almost any white-collar career and a growing number of blue-collar jobs as well, people need to know how to participate in meetings and eventually run them. Realizing the importance of teamwork, most teachers now use student groups for much of their schoolwork, and they realize the need to teach leadership skills so the kids can work effectively in teams. Just as we need to learn these skills, kids do, too.

So what are some strategies to teach group participation and leadership skills?

Teach kids how to run meetings.

Older students can benefit from learning basics of running teams and meetings—creating agendas, taking minutes, using Robert's Rules, and voting or reaching consensus. Participating in mock trials is often popular, as well as model congresses and model United Nations groups with other schools (this was one of Harry's favorite high school experiences). In science class, students can lead research teams.

Give kids time to practice new strategies.

Following minilessons on particular leadership tasks, kids can practice by taking turns leading groups and projects within their classroom and in other classrooms. We can also give students lots of practice in public speaking and debate so they get over their shyness about speaking up in groups.

Have students create goals.

We can ask students to create classroom-level strategic plans for the school year, including both academic and nonacademic goals, broken down by quarters or months. This gets them used to monitoring their own academic development, which will be helpful as they work to complete longer class projects and research papers.

Expose students to careers that showcase teamwork.

We can teach students about the everyday lives of professionals in a variety of careers. Students can shadow adults at their jobs for a morning and visit workplaces of different kinds, where they are sure to witness teamwork in action.

Not every student will become a leader, just as not all will become mathematicians or artists, but at least more kids will gain leadership experience, and those who are not learning these skills at home—or from the Scouts, debate team, or other extracurricular organizations—will get some practice. More colleges and universities now explicitly offer leadership courses, so why not start teaching these skills early? A by-product will be that student teams will work more effectively in all of our classrooms.

WHAT PRINCIPALS CAN DO

It would be hard to overstate the principal's role in supporting teachers' collaboration on teams and committees. Teachers (and indeed most organizations' workers) are famous for their ability to resist top-down decisions by closing their doors and teaching as they see fit, so building participation rather than trying to force compliance is a more effective way to achieve real change. Encouraging teacher's self-directed, professional development in leadership, organization, and project management skills will prepare them to be effective at participating in and running teams to improve the school. Without these skills, distribution of responsibilities can end up in wasted opportunities and disappointing results. Important ways to show respect for the teaching staff through committee work:

- *Include teachers in decisions* about professional development instead of imposing sit-and-git workshops.

- *Provide time and space* for collaboration by arranging schedules that include common prep time. If the whole school can have some time to work together once a week or bimonthly to pursue collaborative projects, so much the better. Achieve this by letting school out a little early or starting a little later once a week; this shows teachers how much the principal respects their work. Then when it comes time to ask for help, people will trust the motivation for that request.

- *Be clear on the mandate* for a particular task, including outcomes and deadline dates.

- *Allow easy access to technology* to facilitate documentation of committee work.

● *Include teachers on important projects* like new faculty searches and school-wide initiatives—efforts to improve communication with parents, the board, or the community, for example. This can create the kind of collaborative atmosphere that is an essential ingredient of a vibrant school culture.

9 | Mount a Campaign

How It Helps You

When some issue really needs to be addressed at your school and you decide to try taking action, think of your effort as a campaign—a set of strategies with a beginning, middle, and end. Community organizers approach projects this way all the time. If you are ready to get more involved in the professional life of your school, and a larger project is crying to be attempted, what steps will give you the greatest chance for success? The last thing you'd want to do is try, fail, and become discouraged, along with your fellow teachers. Simply complaining rarely works. Showing leadership means acting strategically and productively.

Janine Givens-Belsley taught for several years at a small K–8 school that, amazingly, had no planning periods for teachers whatsoever. Kids were even in the classrooms during lunch. So Janine sketched out a schedule that would incorporate an hour of planning time for every teacher at least four days per week, using a modest amount of funding to pay for some elective courses and aides. Before starting her campaign, Janine checked with the principal, who was mildly interested but noncommittal—enough clearance for her to begin her campaign.

Next, Janine consulted fellow faculty members in her own department—grades 7 and 8—where she had strong relationships. Then she branched out, first with people she knew fairly well. But outside her grade level, links were not strong between cultural groups, so others on her team helped pave the way. As she met with people, she asked how each one viewed the problem, to make sure the plan fit that person's needs, and made adjustments as necessary. Because Janine was busy at the same time working on a successful campaign to add a one-week spring break, a colleague volunteered to work out the details of the schedule.

When Janine next went back to the principal, she was able to state that all the teachers were on board, knowing that he liked to keep his staff unified. The whole thing didn't take all that long; her campaign started in December, and the new schedule, written up by her fellow teacher, was accepted and took effect in January. We should mention one prequel to this story: At a previous school, Janine had drawn up a petition for fewer preps, with no advance warning for the principal. He angrily rejected the request, saying she was ungrateful for all his hard work. Lesson learned.

Make It Work

Initiating change in a school almost always requires more than just a petition or a motivational speaker. Think of it as a process that requires careful strategizing based on the attitudes, history, groupings of teachers, and leadership styles in your building. What resources and support will you need? What goal is realistic? Aim for something achievable, but don't underestimate the possibilities or assume people will react negatively. If you make the right moves, you may get a lot further than you expect. Here are some important steps.

Do your research.

It's important to be well armed with information to back up your proposal. So gather information; locate relevant articles or books, local experts at universities or school reform organizations, data on student needs, and examples of successful applications at other schools that teachers could visit.

Focus your objective.

A faculty can accomplish a limited number of major improvements in a school year. Consider how your project fits within the school's main priorities, mission, and goals and whether you will have to give up time for something else in order to concentrate on this new plan. Your project needs to be allied closely enough with the school's goals that you have a chance of winning administrative support and important enough that you and the other teachers will be willing to set aside other projects to focus on this one. Many "Christmas tree" schools are decked with initiatives but never achieve the critical mass to get any one of them solidly established. You don't want that.

Acquire outside help.

It's important to know in advance what resources you'll need, what they may cost, and where funds might come from. There's a surprising amount of help out there. Facing History and Ourselves, for example, provides some workshops on teaching about social issues and responsibility at no cost, while fees are required for others. School leaders and teachers regularly call Steve at the Illinois Writing Project to inquire about workshops to support literacy development at their schools. The project's summer leadership institutes actually pay teachers a stipend, while workshops at schools usually cost money. On the funding side, we help you think about grants and partnerships in Chapters 12 and 13.

At the Young Women's Leadership Charter School, in Chicago, Kristi Eilers, the teacher in charge of professional development, uncovered a problem that she knew would take some resources to solve. At this school, each teacher defines outcomes students must meet in order to pass her course. This is part of a system to help ensure that all students succeed, since they and their teachers are able to go back and make up the kids' "not yet's." Kristi realized that there were inconsistencies in the outcomes from grade to grade. While some teachers were showing juniors how to organize essays, for example, others were covering the topic in seventh grade. A more coherent sequence of outcomes was needed across grade levels. The main resource for addressing this incoherence was time, so the school director, Margaret Small, agreed to pay for two Saturday work sessions for five teachers. The team also elicited help from an education professor, Jennifer Cohen, and from Mary Ann Pitcher, a former school codirector—and the job got done.

Talk it through.

We described how Janine Givens-Belsley talked with every teacher in the school before going fully public with her proposal. Chapter 7, "Speak Up," helps you think through the various steps in this process. A brief summary:

- *Check in with the principal.* Pique his interest with a relevant article, or show how the topic is tied to an issue you know he's concerned about.

- *Lay the groundwork* by talking with both supporters and skeptics (but don't go to the doubters so early that they scotch the whole effort).

● *Line up supporters beforehand* who will back you up if you're presenting your idea at a meeting.

Plan for implementation.

Think in advance about the steps needed to bring your project to fruition:

● Should you propose that the whole school take on the project or that it start with a pilot department, grade level, or group of volunteers?

● Can all the parts of the work be tackled at once, or should it be planned and executed in stages?

● Should the project be introduced by an outside expert or by internal colleagues?

● Will materials, lesson plans, guidebooks, or other supports be needed?

At Al Raby School for Community and Environment, a committee led by assistant principal Jim Schwartz (now the principal) sought to promote collaborative learning throughout the school. A consultant led a workshop on the topic, and the committee compiled a short manual to guide implementation. But the effort didn't catch fire. A fresh committee with stronger commitment among its members gave it a second-year try. They recruited four volunteer teachers from various subject areas to first visit classrooms in several other schools where collaborative activities were the norm and then develop model classrooms. In the spring other Raby teachers planned to observe the volunteers piloting the collaborative models. The project is still advancing, but everyone is much happier with its progress, now that there is a more defined process for spreading the approach across the school.

Consider how to help people work together.

In our experience (and in studies by groups like the Consortium on Chicago School Research – see Sebring *et al.*, 2006), the success of an improvement project depends mightily on the relationships among the adults in the school. Trust among colleagues is essential. If a team is working on your project, do its members work well together? Do they need to set some norms for discussion and decision making? Will others in the school give the project a fair hearing? If there are problems or glitches, can people talk constructively and resolve them? It's useful to enlist the support of influential colleagues who can actively help ensure affirmative answers to these questions. But you'll also want to

Show-Off?

When we step up in the professional community, colleagues can sometimes think we're trying to show them up, even though we have not intended that. Teachers especially experience this in a school where little initiative is encouraged and most of the faculty members keep quiet in meetings. Obviously, if almost everyone were taking on a role, a single person's actions simply wouldn't stand out.

Getting Over It

Mary Beth Werner, a teacher at Telpochcalli School, takes on tasks beyond her own classroom, but has sometimes worried about how her colleagues perceive her. One of her most valued supports, she explained, is her relationship with fellow teacher Irma Jimenez. Irma has been a mentor for Mary Beth, a person she can talk to when sensitive issues come up. As a young, progressive, and—as she herself says—"chatty" teacher, she was concerned that she could seem pushy. But her talks with Irma reassured her that her contributions would be valued. Now, several years later, she mentors new teachers at the school, just as Irma had done for her—though through collaborative efforts rather than a formal program.

ensure that your team uses an effective process for getting work done. There's more on this in Chapter 8, "Deal with Committees."

Maintain momentum.

Once a project is under way, it can be challenging to keep everything on track. Crises and other projects intervene. People wear down over the course of the year. Not everyone in the building may share your level of enthusiasm. Testing brings everything else to a halt. What do you need to do to keep things going?

- *Consider regular, short news bulletins*, either through email or faculty mailboxes.

- *Talk up your project* at meetings. Share promising results, and get input from people on issues to be addressed or adjustments needed.

- *Check in regularly*. Communicate thoroughly with everyone and hold brief check-ins with key people, so no problem simmers for long without receiving attention.

- *Don't postpone meetings*, even if not every committee member can attend. Email those who can't come, to get input, share deliberations, and keep things moving.

- *Most important, draw up a time line* with deadlines for everyone so that you can plan backward from your goal, know when you're on or off track, and reconfigure the plan when necessary.

Assess your progress.

Assessment has taken on woefully negative associations, with standardized tests used to label schools and narrow the focus of the curriculum. But data gathering doesn't need to be destructive or just an afterthought add-on. Nor is good information obtained only through tests. If you and your fellow teachers work hard on a project, it would obviously be good to learn if it was worthwhile, to own the bragging rights, to encourage people onward, and to see what further improvements might be needed.

At Telpochcalli School, the faculty worked a full year on a new framework for dual language teaching that is the centerpiece of their curriculum and then spent a second year implementing the new framework. Teachers' end-of-year written reflections were invaluable for celebrating the successes, identifying what problems still needed attention (teachers didn't hesitate to bring these up), and determining what to do next. A few typical observations that helped everyone understand how far the project had progressed:

- We have begun to have consistency/continuity in our bilingual program where teachers know when to teach what language. It has also started us focusing on assessment.

- Teachers know what language (English or Spanish) will be used in every grade and subject matter. The groups have discussed useful assessment tools that are being used and hopefully will be used throughout the school so we have a common tool to refer to.

- We need to work on mapping the content for ESL/SSL throughout the grades. We also need to know what materials (programs, music, and so on) are used in every grade.

- I would love to have a workshop specific to bilingual social education.

In the Classroom

Campaigns that accomplish some real result out in the world can be especially powerful for students. They're engaging and show the kids how their learning can actually make a difference. Jeff Hoyer conducts just such projects in his environmental science classes at Deerfield High School. Students research ecological problems around the world and then propose projects to the class to help address them. The class chooses which project to tackle and gets to work. Student fund-raising activities may be involved, along with further research, letter writing, and follow-up to learn about the results of their efforts. For a recent project, students chose the problem of unsanitary drinking water in the country of Mali. Health issues like this are a major source of disease around the world. The kids raised money to help a nonprofit agency purchase new water pumping equipment by selling low-energy lightbulbs, recycling old cell phones, and holding garage sales. As a result, Mali villagers were able to dig wells to provide a safe water supply for the first time (Daniels, Zemelman, and Steineke 2007, 218–20).

There are many other creative ways to connect curriculum to action in the wider world. English and reading classes can write stories and reviews and actually circulate them to promote literacy and love of literature. Xian Barrett's social studies students in Chicago conducted a letter-writing campaign to promote awareness of the continuing violence at their school, and the major newspapers picked up the story. Math classes can use statistics to analyze and promote more responsible behavior in areas such as traffic safety or healthy eating. Projects like these are time-consuming. But they are highly memorable and help students make lifelong commitments to the subjects we love. When we contacted one of Jeff Hoyer's students after she'd graduated and headed off to college, she told us she'd decided to major in environmental studies as a result of her experience in his class.

WHAT PRINCIPALS CAN DO

Principals need to support the campaigns of teachers who passionately seek to improve the school. They need the commitment of these leaders to make the school great, because the job cannot be accomplished by just one person at the top. The principal may need to encourage teachers to focus projects on the big priorities for improvement that the school has adopted but at the same time draw on their particular passions and energies. Many of these teacher leaders will benefit from coaching to help them become skilled and successful. It's important to meet with them periodically to discuss how their projects are going and find out what challenges they are encountering. And as the projects gain the support of faculty, the principal can provide resources and public assurances of approval at key points to help them get off the ground.

This has been Amy Rome's approach for the past three years in her principalship at the National Teachers Academy, a neighborhood school in Chicago that is also a teacher training site. Amy has encouraged shared leadership throughout the school, while at the same time pressing teachers to strengthen their individual practice and the school's instructional programs. When teachers take on wider roles, Amy asserted, it not only helps the school but also improves their own teaching.

Amy is particularly proud of the leadership by her two literacy teachers, who guided the redesign of the school's reading program. They began their campaign with plenty of consultation and listening to their colleagues. They administered self-assessments, conducted walk-throughs that included fellow teachers, provided help with tasks like creating classroom libraries of leveled books, co-taught classes, and held coaching sessions.

In this example, the teachers held more formal leadership roles than others we've described, but the principal's role as coach is what is instructive here. Every day, Amy figures, she met with the literacy teachers for at least a few minutes. She observed and provided feedback on the individual meetings they held with the classroom teachers. She modeled effective behaviors and strategies herself, such as how to work in a nonauthoritarian and constructive way with teachers who were reluctant to make changes. And she consulted with them on other issues to provide a larger perspective on the school and their work within it.

Amy also signaled her full support for their efforts. At first, she needed to restate this explicitly in response to each of the steps that the literacy teachers proposed. But as the program redesign took root, she found that everyone in the building recognized that she supported it. One other necessity: Amy sought out a coach for herself, as she realized how complex and challenging this kind of effort could be. And a note on the resulting success: reading scores have gone up 22 percent over the past two years.

10 | Talk to the Man

How It Helps You

Some of us feel comfortable walking in to hang out with the superintendent, principal, or assistant principal. Others would rather have a root canal than have to say more than "Good morning" and "Bye-bye" to her, let alone sit and schmooze in her office. Of course, there are many leadership styles exercised by principals, in all manner of settings. Yours may be a school where you *can* chat with your school leader every day. Or you may be in a large building where you hardly ever see her, except at big, formal faculty meetings. Your principal may linger in the halls every morning or hunker down in her office dealing with paperwork all day. Your approach will depend on her mode of operating, as well as your own. Yet the principal is your boss, the person officially responsible for the school. Sooner or later, if you're expanding your role as a teacher and building your career, you'll need to work constructively with this person.

Working with a school leader is part strategy and part attitude. Growing as a teacher leader involves developing not just the confidence to connect with people outside your own area of responsibility, but the thoughtful understanding of what the world looks like to others. Kids, parents, administrators, building engineers—all live in their own particular worlds, and it helps to be able to understand their responsibilities, challenges, and life-shaping experiences. It broadens your understanding of the world around you. And skill in communicating well with people who may seem challenging will not only get you more of what you need in order to do your job effectively, but also make you feel more at home in your building and provide more options in your professional career.

Make It Work

Let's think through some of the steps that can help you work effectively with your principal. Perhaps you simply want to build the relationship so that when the time comes to make a request, you have this person's trust and know you will get a fair hearing; you may have a specific need for which you require support right away; or there may be an issue that you'd like to be able to resolve constructively. We can take a look at strategies for all of these.

First, establish an ongoing practice of communicating.

It's a lot harder to bring up a problem if you've talked to the principal only at your hiring interview and in evaluation sessions. Without some in-depth conversation, you won't know much about the boss' style or interests, and he won't know about yours. Each of you would instead be relying mainly on mental images created out of fragmentary information. But if your important talk is part of an ongoing dialogue, it can be more natural as well as better planned.

The most essential approach—and one that we've come back to repeatedly in this book—is the one-on-one conversation. It's intentionally designed to help you and the other party build an understanding of and appreciation for each person's background and values. Of course, for a principal deluged with work, it may be harder than with others to schedule an open-ended sit-down. So you may need to get started by going in with a more concrete item—seeking advice about a student who is struggling or asking whether the principal knows of issues in the student's family that you should be aware of, for example. You can then tag on a short beginning to a more in-depth conversation: "While I'm here, do you mind my asking: I've heard a little about your experience with teaching math in the past, but then you moved into administration. I'm wondering whether I should consider a move like that down the road. I'd like to hear about how you decided to do that." Most people enjoy talking about their experiences, so you're likely to elicit a positive response. On the other hand, you might want to offer to help the principal with one of his projects: "I heard that you're planning to start a parent communication committee. That's the kind of work I'd enjoy doing." This shows that you are thinking about the principal's needs as well as your own and are willing to be a team player. Either of these two openings can make it easier to schedule a follow-up discussion.

If you're in a larger school with a more distant leader, letter writing or emailing may be the way to get discussion started. Our friend Mark Larson made a practice of writing letters—to his district superintendent, to colleagues, and to students—in order to start conversations about big issues in his teaching and in the school. Of course recipients couldn't resist responding with their own thoughts and ideas. All of this eventually evolved into Larson's book *Making Conversation: Collaborating with Colleagues for Change* (1997).

Do a little research.

Nowadays it is far easier to learn about a person's background than it used to be, with a Google web page never far from your fingertips. Mark Larson's superintendent when he was at Evanston Township High School was Allan Alson. While both Larson and Alson have moved on to other work, a little online searching tells us some key facts about this former school leader:

- Alson was a founder of the Minority Student Achievement Network, an organization of high schools across the country working on improving minority students' success.

- Back in 1993, Alson supported a local effort on gun control in Evanston.

- He's on the board of directors of the National Society for the Study of Education, which was founded by John Dewey.

- He more recently served as director of the High School Transformation Project, a Chicago Public Schools initiative to improve the city's high schools.

School board meeting minutes will also yield plenty of information about the issues a school leader has addressed. Obviously, knowing about the principal's concerns and passions can help immensely as you develop the relationship or prepare to make a specific request.

Examine your own thoughts, needs, and style of relating.

What is most important to you, in your professional life? What are the strengths that you bring to the table? What kinds of information and perspectives might your boss appreciate, that she may not know about? We're not talking about becoming the principal's pet or crony. But it's not a bad thing for her to realize that you can be an important resource for the school.

There are deeper attitudinal questions as well. What are your own responses to authority that you might need to set aside so you can go in to the principal, listen openly, and make suggestions? If the stakes are high—as when you are making an important request or bringing up a sensitive issue—this becomes especially significant, because you will need to stay focused on what you really need from the exchange. Sometimes we are so worried that a listener will shoot down our ideas that we actually censor ourselves. You'll see in an upcoming story that though Lorena Kramer came to teaching feeling comfortable working with her bosses, she nevertheless assumed, mistakenly, that her principal would refuse to spend money on the technological equipment she wanted. Fortunately, Lorena still worked up the nerve to ask.

Steve realized the role of his own expectations a number of years ago, when he wanted a leave of absence from his teaching position in order to help start a new small high school in Chicago. He hesitated to make the request for fear that his dean would be angry or insulted. But a friend encouraged Steve to ask himself, "What's the worst that could happen?" and in his particular situation, the answer was "Not much, really." His request, when he made it, was promptly granted. Of course, if you believe your risk level is higher—perhaps your job is not secure or your principal tends to become defensive easily—you'll need to prepare the ground more extensively before you bring up your issue.

Make a specific request.

We talked in Chapter 7, on speaking up, about preparing yourself with research and consultation with fellow teachers, so we needn't revisit that here. But there are many ways to approach the principal when you are ready to do so. Will you be direct or start tentatively? Will you present your ideas right away or ask for her thoughts first: "I know our students have been struggling on the reading tests, and I was wondering what you think is behind that and how we could address it?" Listening first is good. At the same time, you don't want to appear weak or tentative. Complaining rarely goes over well, either, so be positive and focus on what your request can accomplish *for the kids*—and by extension, for the principal.

Lorena Kramer's story shows how the process can work at its best. Lorena, whom we discussed in Chapter 3, had previously been a chemical engineer for Saturn, where automotive manufacturing was revolutionized with a team approach. Assembly-line problems there were solved by nonhierarchical teams composed of line workers, engineers, and managers. So when Lorena became a math teacher at a large urban school, it was second nature for her to go to her department chair and principal with her concerns.

The first issue she tackled was her students' need for graphing calculators. The school had been providing only simpler scientific calculators and only during high-stakes exams, so the students naturally spent much precious exam time playing with their new toys. Realizing that these kids could perform well only after plenty of practice, she pleaded with her department chair to furnish calculators for all math students—and furthermore for these to be the more sophisticated graphing version. But such a large purchase was beyond the chair's power, so Lorena took the bold step of going directly to the principal, though she worried that she'd meet resistance. She was surprised that her five-minute plea received a simple response: "Well, order some."

Two years later, under a new principal, and now serving as math department chair, Lorena found herself again in the principal's office. This time, it was the principal who bemoaned the lackluster state of the school's technology. Lorena, just back from a demonstration of Smart Board™ interactive whiteboards, asked, "Are you really serious about this? If so, you should get Smart Boards™ for all of the classrooms. The only problem is that they cost a thousand dollars apiece." Again, Lorena was amazed at the answer: "Sure, let's get some." Unfortunately, when Lorena went to order the boards, she found that the ones she wanted actually cost four thousand apiece! Embarrassed and nervous, she went back to the principal to admit her mistake. Her response: "Oh, then let's get only twenty to start." In the year since, the boards clearly helped improve math instruction, so the principal later committed to furnish them for other departments as well. It turned out to be a win-win situation in which everyone came out looking good.

An advantage of taking the sometimes difficult step of going to the principal the first time is that each successive trip becomes easier, because you now know and therefore hopefully trust each other a little. Lorena asked for other equipment, and though she was sometimes refused, she didn't take no for a final answer. Instead, she amassed more evidence and returned to argue that the purchases would raise student achievement, improve faculty morale, and make the principal and the school look good. Most recently she successfully campaigned for data analysis software to help teachers pinpoint instructional needs, and the teachers now appreciate the focus it gives to team and department meetings.

One double-edged development is that Lorena now has to perform tasks for the principal that she sometimes does not relish, like ordering furniture for classrooms, but she realizes that if she wants to continue to have the principal's ear, she has to be cognizant of the principal's needs as well as her own. And Lorena finds her job much more rewarding now that she can see the benefits for her colleagues and their students. Teachers say that they stay at the school because of the camaraderie Lorena and others have fostered, and for the first time students at this large urban high school are now taking a pre-calculus course as well as AP calculus. A few are even doing well enough on the AP exam to win college credit—a direct outgrowth of the school's technological advances and Lorena's leadership.

Be prepared when bringing up a sensitive issue.

Now comes the hard part. If you have a trusting bond with the principal and feel confident that the two of you can handle a tough controversy or misunderstanding, that's great. But sometimes when the stakes are high, even people who've worked together for a long time need some well-structured techniques for keeping the dialogue constructive and moving it toward a positive outcome. And if you don't have a strong relationship, you'll need those techniques even more. A guide that we've found extremely helpful and that we recommended in Chapter 5 is the book *Crucial Conversations*, by Kerry Patterson and coauthors Joseph Grenny, Ron McMillan, and Al Switzler (2002).

Two concepts from this book stand out, in our experience. One is to focus on the core outcomes you want to achieve, so you can avoid becoming sidetracked or hung up on negative matters that don't actually move the discussion forward. This can keep you from becoming defensive or accusatory, responses that are likely to shut down the dialogue. The second concept is to help people to feel safe. In order to really work on a problem, the person you are talking with needs to feel respected and not blamed. You will want to help him become a partner in the process of straightening out the issue, rather than an adversary.

We can see how both of these concepts could have helped if that principal had been more resistant to our friend Lorena's request for graphing calculators. What if she had argued that Lorena needed to teach more effectively and the calculators were just an excuse for her lack of success? Arguing back might have helped Lorena feel more righteous, but it would very likely have put her principal on the defensive—not a good state of mind for agreeing to those calculators. Her better response would be to step back and focus on their shared goal—increasing student learning and performance—and ask how they could work together to achieve that. The principal naturally would need to feel safe and respected in her role, or she would be more concerned with defending herself or attacking Lorena than with the teachers' and kids' needs.

There's plenty more to learn in order to be constructive and successful in negotiations like this, and *Crucial Conversations* can walk you through more of the process. Some practice and experience will be important as well. Life tends to offer plenty of opportunities for that.

In the Classroom

Young children do not hesitate to approach teachers about conflicts with their classmates: "He keeps taking my pencils!" But students of all ages sometimes hesitate to ask for help when they don't understand something. And especially with complex tasks like math application problems or writing assignments, they're not always clear on what specific help they need. An important part of our work, then, is to help students learn to communicate constructively with teachers and ask for help in a useful way. Classrooms and schools in which students feel comfortable talking to the teachers and administrators about issues have a more relaxed atmosphere; they resemble healthy families. Following are some strategies for building this kind of climate in your classroom.

Model vulnerability.

Kids enjoy spotting the teacher's own mistakes, particularly if she is composing a piece of writing or completing a problem on an overhead or Smart Board™ interactive whiteboard. Suddenly they become great spellers and math calculators. Include a few errors on purpose, if you're not already a little error prone yourself. And regularly ask the students to check over your work to make sure you got it right. It's important to talk about this explicitly: Making a mistake is not a bad thing. Everyone does it. What's important is how you seek help and how you learn from it. This will also enable you to see if your kids have internalized the skills and the proofreading or problem-checking strategies you have taught them.

Have students look over their work before asking for help.

As a class, practice reviewing a volunteer's sample draft on the overhead. Use the lessons that you teach on specific concepts and strategies to help students learn to recognize for themselves when they've done something well and when the outcome still needs work. Make this a regular part of the process of writing compositions, solving math problems, completing exercises, writing up lab reports, and completing big projects. Students must develop the habit of revising if they are to become comfortable making mistakes and learning from them, rather than continuing to turn in sloppy or obsessively perfect first drafts. Of course, to make revisions or to get help with them, the writer needs to learn how to look at her work and identify the parts that could most benefit from improvement. Similarly with math, students can learn about problem-solving processes to help them pinpoint where they've gone wrong or at what stage they've gotten stuck, so they can intelligently ask for help.

Develop your own constructive use of language with students.

Teachers are sometimes quick to blame kids in a generalized way when things get out of hand. We're human, and it's easy to do when the day has been long and the kids are getting on your last nerve. Many good teachers we know have worked to develop language and tone that effectively guides students in positive directions, instead of simply becoming confrontational. But to alter ingrained habits, one needs not only good intentions but intentional practice using specific, well-conceived ways of talking and responding. *The Power of Our Words*: *Teacher Language That Helps Children Learn*, by Paula Denton (2007), is a great tool to help with this process. In fact, at one school, teachers have paired up to observe each other in their classrooms, specifically to help refine the way they talk to students in challenging situations. This approach will make the classroom a positive place where kids feel safe asking for what they need.

WHAT PRINCIPALS CAN DO

We've heard the statement many times: "I have an open-door policy." A principal who is serious about encouraging input from teachers needs to go much further than that. We've talked about one-on-one meetings with teachers to actively solicit their thinking, signal openness, and establish a regular pattern of communication (see Chapter 5, "Build Bridges"). And we've talked about steps for building trust (see Chapter 7, "Speak Up"). One well-structured way to solicit teachers' ideas is to use a professional development session in which teacher teams (by grade level or subject area) review data or student work and report out the strengths and weaknesses that they see. Of course, the data needs to be sufficiently useful and analytical to pinpoint specifics. Overall scores on a state test don't provide such information, and even when they are disaggregated, they may still be of little use in identifying the particular skills that students need help with. So be sure the information is more specific than that.

At Northwest Middle School, in Chicago, principal Marilyn Strojny asked the teachers in each subject area to create and administer a common diagnostic assessment. Then in grade-level teams, the teachers identified patterns that they saw and discussed how these might apply across the different subjects. The reports from the teams provided the school's instructional leadership team with valuable evidence to help it choose a focus for improvement across the school. As a great side benefit, the teachers especially appreciated having the time and an organized way to talk among their team members and compare the needs that they saw in their own classrooms. "We never get the time to do this," they said. "Can we schedule another round again soon?"

Reach Outside

Reach Out to Parents | *11*

How It Helps You

Every school is an intense universe all its own—including the unremitting demands, the kids and all their needs, the relationships with colleagues, the lesson planning, the paperwork, the mandates, and the meetings and committees. Sometimes it can be hard to maintain connection with anything beyond the four walls of your room or your building (just ask our spouses). At the same time, parents, school boards, politicians, news media, and all manner of forces press on us and define our work, even as some of them also offer tremendous opportunities to enrich it. If we ignore these forces, we risk becoming passive pawns, shuffled around the chessboard of the education world. If we reach out to the wider world, we strengthen ourselves as teachers and build authentic power.

The most immediate members of the outside world for us are parents. When we connect with them, our work is easier and our children's learning becomes more productive. They can help us understand the support networks and struggles that kids are experiencing at home and the history and baggage they bring with them to school every day.

Make It Work

Perhaps the greatest challenge with parents is not about guiding them to support their children's learning, as important as that is. Rather, it is figuring out how to build trusting relationships with them—especially given the intensely personal nature of family life. As with so much we've described in this book, building trust is central. When it's lacking, parents and teachers often end up viewing each other as adversaries. Here are some ways you can work to break down this barrier.

Listen closely.

Harry remembers when, during a parent-teacher conference, a parent asked angrily why he assigned so much African American literature in his AP English class. Assuming that this parent, a white woman, was opposed to multiculturalism, Harry tried to explain that literary inclusiveness was especially important in a school with such a large African American population. After ten minutes of attempts to mollify her, he suddenly realized from a comment she dropped that she was Latina and was objecting to the lack of Latino material. Once he understood this, he was able to reassure her of his awareness and respect for this literature. He promised to recommend some Latino authors to students, and the two of them found common ground. Lesson learned: listen closely to parents' agendas so that you are communicating rather than speaking past each other.

Share stories.

First-grade teacher Karen Hankins, in her book *Teaching Through the Storm: A Journal of Hope* (2003), describes a tougher moment, when the mother of a child with learning disabilities confronted her at the start of the school year:

> "Look . . . I never met you. I don't even know your name. But you are my enemy. I hate you and everybody connected to this school and any other school for what you are trying to do to my baby, my precious child."
>
> . . . I felt her anger growing at least as fast as my fear. I would not be able to talk to her as a teacher. I had to meet her mother to mother. (2–4)

This gulf was not of Hankins' making, but she still had to face it. And how did she manage? Through stories she and this distraught mother shared about their own families. Hankins described the struggles her own family faced trying to obtain good schooling for her sister, who had suffered brain damage, and these stories ultimately built a strong working relationship between teacher and parent.

Jo Beth Allen, in her wise and useful *Creating Welcoming Schools: A Practical Guide to Home-School Partnerships with Diverse Families* (2007), explores a wide range of strategies for building school-parent relationships. Allen strongly urges us to start by sharing stories in individual parent-teacher conferences and larger parent-night meetings—stories of good experiences in school and stories of bad or painful ones, stories about ourselves, and experiences with our own children. Teachers will have negative ones just as the parents do, along with the upbeat tales that show what school can be at its best. These stories not only provide teachers insight into the family's attitude toward school, but also build trust by placing teachers and family members on the same footing and showing that teachers understand the challenges families face.

Organize parent projects or activities.

In *More than Bake Sales*: *The Resource Guide for Family Involvement in Education* (1998), Jim Vopat focuses especially on organizing "parent projects." These are workshops that bring parents together to build relationships, address needs at the school, and understand their kids' learning by experiencing some of it themselves. Parents read books in literature circles, just as their kids do in class (39–46). They write letters addressing problems in their neighborhood (21–23). And teachers and parents write back and forth to each other in dialogue journals (47–54). Again, the sharing of personal stories builds the bridge. Ultimately, the projects build leadership among the parents themselves.

Here are some of the other activities that Jo Beth Allen and Jim Vopat recommend for parent-teacher partnerships, along with several of our own pointers for carrying them out. Some may involve the whole school, or a team, while others can be initiated on your own.

- *Cultural memoirs*. Parents and teachers write and share memoirs focused on their own childhood experiences. One way to get started is to ask parents to draw maps of their childhood neighborhood and then talk in small groups about memories associated with the various spots they've represented (an effective prewriting strategy for kids, too, of course). Focusing on a single relative is another way in. For parents not comfortable with writing, you can provide note cards on which they simply list words and phrases.

- *Family histories*. Invite children, family members, and teachers to compose family histories. These can include family trees, pictures, interviews, and research into countries of origin. One guide for such a project is *History Comes Home*: *Family Stories Across the Curriculum*, written by Steve and a team of fellow educators (Zemelman et al. 2000). Jo Beth Allen explains how Tucson teacher Cathy Amanti discovered through kids' family studies that many owned horses, enabling her to base classroom activities on kids' knowledge about caring for them. Allen, Amanti, and fellow educators have created the Family Funds of Knowledge Project to pursue this work. It's described in *Funds of Knowledge: Theorizing Practices in Households, Communities, and Classrooms*, by Norma Gonzales, Luis Moll, and Cathy Amanti (2005).

● *Home visits.* Allen describes a project in rural Kentucky in which teachers visited children's families repeatedly over the school year. These visits revealed "which families helped with homework and which thought it was the school's job; emotional and academic needs that might not be evident at school; and family knowledge such as farming procedures. . . . This information influenced myriad teaching decisions" (2007, 47–48). Home visits involve plenty of challenges, of course—time limited to after-school hours, lack of resources to pay for the effort, conflicts between building parents' trust versus the occasional responsibility to share information about serious family problems.

Jo Beth Allen and other educators describe many more strategies for engaging families, some easier to implement and others more expansive, some more practical in elementary schools and others equally possible in high schools:

● getting-to-know-you conferences at the start of the year

● student-led parent conferences, using portfolios to review kids' work

● student-written classroom newspapers to let parents know what their kids are doing

● hand-off chats, where teachers talk with parents as they pick up kids at the end of the day

● family literacy nights that include kids and parents reading to each other

● suppers for kids, teachers, and families together

● home reading journals

● parent resource centers in schools

● projects on wider community needs, such as access to health and family support services

A useful guide for taking a team through the planning process for one or more of these strategies is *Partnerships by Design: Cultivating Effective and Meaningful School-Family-Community Partnerships*, by Debbie Ellis and Kendra Hughes

Collaborating Effectively

How can we approach the development of parent-teacher relationships in the most strategic way possible—and then encourage this among our colleagues? Anne Henderson and Karen Mapp, in *A New Wave of Evidence: The Impact of School, Family, and Community Connections on Student Achievement* (2002), identify common elements of effective parent involvement programs from the eighty studies on parent-school relationships that they reviewed:

- They invite involvement, are welcoming, and address specific parental and community needs.

- They engage diverse families, recognize cultural and class differences, address these needs directly, and build on cultural strengths.

- They embrace a partnership philosophy in which power is shared: the responsibility for children's educational development is a collaborative enterprise among parents, school staff, and community members.

(2002). Another is the Center for Education and the Study of Diverse Populations' website Working Together: School-Family-Community Partnerships—a Toolkit for New Mexico School Communities, which connects the viewer to a wide range of further online resources (www.ped.state.nm.us/div/rural_ed /toolkit/index.html). It may well be that one of these types of partnership projects could provide just the focus for bringing fellow teachers together as a team, deepening your own relationships as a faculty, and expanding everyone's sense of the possibilities within your professional community.

Maia Golley, the first-grade teacher at Namaste School, admitted that in her first job at her previous school, she "avoided the children's parents as much as possible. It was difficult to contact them, and when encounters did occur, they acted abusively" (evidence, sadly, that the school had failed overall to develop relationships with parents and instead held them at arm's length). At Namaste, it has been a far different story. Maia and her co-teacher started off by conducting once-per-trimester activities for the families—workshops on math, read-alouds along with explanations of how to hold conversations with children about books, and book giveaways. While the parents responded very positively, she acknowledged that it was still a challenge to reach those whose children needed help the most. So she began holding less formal after-school coffee sessions and has planned to start a parent book club. When one strategy doesn't do the whole job, a smart teacher designs another.

The level of parents' trust that we begin with varies widely from one school and neighborhood to the next and from one individual family to another. It tends to be much lower in neighborhoods of lower economic status. But the weight of our responsibility for people's children is always present. As Shelley Harwayne once declared in a talk (July 2005), "Every parent with a child in school has a piece of their heart living outside their body."

In the Classroom

Many parent and family connections are directly tied to the classroom. Sharon West, who teaches fourth grade at Hurley School, literally brings parents into her classroom not just as volunteer helpers but as learners. If a child has frequent struggles with behavior or homework completion, she'll inquire to see if a parent is available during the day. She'll have him or her (fathers have done this as well as mothers) sit right next to the child during lessons and provide direct help. At first, she said, "the kid soaks it up," though after a while the student would rather cooperate than have a parent around all the time. Sharon values this process for a number of reasons. The parent learns what's involved in the subjects being taught, and Sharon discovers that some of her parents have had little schooling themselves. The parents appreciate being given the tools that enable them to help their kids with homework. Sharon also gets to see how the parent and child interact, which helps her understand what may be going on at home. She compares what she observes with her own struggles and mistakes raising her own kids, and, she explained, this increases her understanding of both arenas.

At Andrew High School in Chicago's south suburbs, teachers of sophomore English, biology, and geometry have teamed up to organize a learning fair project focused on family members (Daniels, Zemelman, and Steineke 2007, 224–35). It combines interviews of family members, the presentation of a speech about a favorite family personality, research on genetic traits in the family, and creation of a scale model of a home or other architectural structure connected with the family. The kids create displays, and family members attend the big event when these are put up at the concluding fair. Obviously, this is a major project that requires extensive planning and coordination. On the other hand, kids and their families remember this project with great fondness for years afterward. And think about what it signals to the parents about the deep connection that's possible between family and school!

WHAT PRINCIPALS CAN DO

Obviously, the principal is in a key position to organize and nurture family and community connections. Principals must make clear that they support the work *and* that it's of great importance. At Legacy Charter School, family engagement was one of four priorities for the 2007–8 school year. Some of the teachers read chapters from *Creating Welcoming Schools* (Allen 2007) to develop a conceptual framework and decide on specific actions for building a more trusting and supportive relationship with the school's families. With the help of a consultant and the support of principal Lisa Kenner, the school held a three-day cycle of workshop sessions (Thursday evening through Saturday afternoon) to begin the process. The first evening, parents joined in small-group roundtable discussions of questions about academics, students' behavior, and school-family communication. They discussed what they knew about the school's efforts in each area and what would help them better support their children. A key element: teachers at each table acted as "silent scribes," listening and taking notes. The next day, the teachers debriefed what they'd heard and participated in a workshop on strategies for building relationships with the families. Saturday morning and afternoon then provided additional roundtable sessions for those unable to attend on Thursday evening. Participation was high and the tables buzzed with intense conversation at each session. Not only did the parents feel they'd been listened to, but teachers received important data on the families' concerns that they could now analyze and use to take action steps. Principals needn't try to do it all, but in this case, Lisa's action made sure this important effort got off the ground.

12 | Get Grants

■ How It Helps You

Let's face it: all teachers could use more resources! Taking action to gain additional monetary support is just one more way that a teacher can reach outside the school walls. And this action not only brings in help for you but also connects you with a wider world. Applying for a grant involves becoming familiar with people and organizations outside of your classroom, which can be energizing in itself and becomes easier the more you do it. You will be forced to explain your ideas to foundation officers, who usually know little about the realities of your work. You'll be educating them and clarifying your own thinking at the same time. And fortunately, grants are more available than you might think.

Justyna Rewilak, first-grade teacher at Lloyd School, wanted to connect with teachers beyond her own building to share her strategies for helping primary-level children create books on the topics they were studying. So she applied to the Chicago Foundation for Education (www.cfegrants.org), which funds teachers to lead study groups on various strategies. On the Web, the foundation lists the topics of all selected teachers so that other Chicago educators can join a group and themselves receive a small stipend for participating. Justyna received one thousand dollars to lead a group on creating children's books for twelve hours of collaborative study over a period of six months. This was Justyna's first foray into leading a group of teachers like this, and she was a bit worried about how she'd do, but she was also excited to try something new and receive recognition for it. Recently, we checked back with Justyna as her workshop series was winding down, and she declared, "Now I know I shouldn't be intimidated about sharing my ideas." When the participants stopped using flat, unexciting writing prompts, and instead asked kids to choose their own topics and create their own books, everyone grew more and more excited about the work. She could see how her own expertise was igniting others' passions, and now she's ready to lead another workshop. Experience is indeed a great teacher, but you'll never have that experience if you don't first take a gamble and write a proposal.

Make It Work

Teachers often imagine troves of money out there somewhere, but where is it, and what do you say in a proposal to convince people to give you some? Most of us don't have a lot of free time to poke around and hesitate to dig into such unknown territory. We'll admit, too, that it takes some serious time and energy to look for these nuggets, so undertaking a search might temporarily replace some other activities we've talked about. You can't do everything at once. But the more possibilities you explore, the more likely you are to find one opportunity that truly ends up providing increased satisfaction in your work.

Let's talk first about what kind of funds are and are not available for teachers' projects. The hard reality about the major foundations: So far in the twenty-first century, most have put their education dollars behind large-scale efforts—in major urban school districts, powerful universities with big-name professors, projects to scale up reforms so they affect large numbers of schools and teachers. Many foundations want their limited funds leveraged through matching commitments from big school districts to multiply the effect of their money, so they aren't excited by "boutique" innovations in a single school. And they want to see quick, measurable results, usually on standardized test scores. Some of us may view this as a shortsighted approach that ignores the way new and exciting ideas actually develop, but it's the reality right now. These conditions will eventually change because fashions in the grant world change, but we're not certain about when.

HOWEVER! There are still many sources of money for teachers—money that is easier to get.

Look for city-based organizations.

Many smaller foundations in cities and towns across the country *do* fund individual teacher efforts. Some examples:

- In Chicago, the Boundless Readers Fund, the Oppenheimer Family Fund, and the Chicago Foundation for Education all give small grants to teachers for exciting work in their own classrooms. Here's what Boundless Readers, for example, says about its grants:

    [Boundless Readers] is a *collaborative peer network for urban educators* that builds teacher expertise and provides classroom resources to inspire teachers and their students to become lifelong readers: individuals who not only *know* how to read, but *do* read. (www.rochelleleefund.org)

    In the eighteen years of its annual awards program, this organization has supported teachers with five thousand awards in 462 Chicago public elementary schools. Through a competitive application process, the fund selects approximately four hundred P–8 classroom teachers each year. Teachers receive up to 150 children's books that *they* select for their classroom library and at least twenty-four hours of professional development designed to promote the effective use of authentic children's books.

- In New York City, the Fund for Teachers partners with schools that are affiliated with a school reform organization, New Visions for Public Schools, to provide small grants to teachers. As their guidelines explain, "Fund for Teachers enriches the personal and professional growth of teachers by recognizing and supporting them as they identify and pursue academic opportunities around the globe . . . The Fund provides fellowship grants [of up to five thousand dollars] directly to teachers with at least three years of experience, to support their professional learning during the summer." (www.fundforteachers/apply/guidelines/ny/newyorkcity/individual/o2.html)

- In Oakland, California, the Fund for Teachers partners with the Marcus A. Foster Educational Institute to provide grants of up to two thousand dollars to Oakland teachers to support creative instruction and professional development.

- In Denver, the Public Education and Business Coalition has most recently been providing grants for teachers in cooperation with the Qwest Foundation and the Fund for Colorado's Future, focusing on innovative uses of technology in the classroom. In fact, the Qwest Foundation has awarded technology grants in fourteen western states.

But big cities are not the only places where support can be found, though sometimes a teacher might need to dig a little to find where it's hidden. For example, in upper New York State, Read to Succeed Buffalo (www .readtosucceedbuffalo.org) advances literacy in schools and neighborhoods. This agency brings together a coalition of fifty nonprofit education groups across the state that offer direct help to schools. While you'll find that Read to Succeed Buffalo doesn't provide grants to teachers, a call to the organization will direct you to a group that can serve your specific needs.

Rural communities, too, provide their share of support. We quickly found the Internet site of the Plus Endowment, in Paris, Tennessee, which provides grants of up to five hundred dollars to individual teachers for special projects. Similarly, the Central Columbia School District, in Bloomsburg, Pennsylvania, houses its own foundation, which collects private donor contributions and then awards five-hundred-dollar grants to individual teachers for projects to improve teaching and learning in their classrooms. Large numbers of local districts and agencies across the country maintain similar programs, and luckily the Web makes it easier to find them than ever before.

Join a professional teacher organization.

You might want to join a local or national teacher professional organization, because many offer grants to their members. Some examples:

- The Illinois Reading Council offers several types of grants for special projects or research. In the 2007–8 academic year, the council gave out fifty-eight thousand dollars in such grants to forty-eight teachers and other school people. Projects ranged from conducting family literacy nights and integrating reading and writing with art and technology to improving reading comprehension and "Shak[ing] Hands with Shakespeare."

- The Colorado Council of the International Reading Association provides three types of grants to individual teachers: Star grants, Teacher as Reader grants, and Teacher as Writer grants. The latter two fund teacher groups rather than individuals.

- The Illinois Council for the Social Studies offers small grants, up to three hundred dollars, to support projects in social studies and history.

● The Michigan Science Teachers Association gave out four one-thousand-dollar mini-grants in 2008.

Check out multinational corporations.

Teachers should not hesitate to ask big multinational corporations for help with funding special projects. According to a *Chicago Tribune* news article on educational innovation (C. Sadovi, May 30, 2008), science teacher David Levine, at Al Raby High School for Community and Environment, obtained a ten-thousand-dollar grant from the oil company BP to guide his chemistry students in refining biodiesel fuel from slimy algae. After the kids test-drove an old Volkswagen camper using the gas they'd made, one enthusiastic junior declared her desire to take up a science career in college.

Search the Web for other sources.

You may be surprised to discover organizations like Adopt-a-Classroom (www.adoptaclassroom.com). At its website you can register to be adopted by an individual donor, who then provides funds to purchase classroom supplies that your school district doesn't provide. Another such website is DonorsChoose.org. If the supplies you desperately need are computers, the U.S. General Services Administration runs the Computers for Learning program, which arranges donations to schools of used computers from government offices; go to http://computersforlearning.gov/ to learn how it works. And the list goes on. Of course, in a better world, education would be more highly valued, and schools would have the money to provide all of the resources for which teachers must now go scrounging. But since we don't live in that world at this time, grants and donations can at least provide us with some of that support—and at the same time connect us with other teachers and educators around the country and the world.

How to Prepare a Successful Grant Application

Review the guidelines carefully.

The first step to preparing a grant application is to look carefully at each foundation's published guidelines. Most will tell you very explicitly what they will and won't fund and what sorts of information they want from you. Steve has

Typical Small-Grant Opportunities for Teachers

- Adopt-a-Classroom

- BP's A+ for Energy program

- Chicago Foundation for Education

- Central Columbia Foundation (school district, Bloomsburg, Pennsylvania)

- Colorado Council of the International Reading Association

- U.S. General Services Administration's Computers for Learning program

- DonorsChoose.org

- Fund for Teachers (partners with programs across the country)

- Illinois Reading Council

- Michigan Science Teachers Association

- Oppenheimer Family Foundation (Chicago)

- Plus Endowment (Paris, Tennessee)

- Boundless Readers Fund (Chicago)

written and reviewed dozens of grant applications over the years, and he's always surprised at how many applicants overlook the directions or qualifying rules published by the target foundation. Here's what the Fund for Teachers has to say about its funding restrictions, for example, that you wouldn't want to miss:

> The Fund awards almost every type of professional development imaginable. However, there are a few exceptions. The Fund will not provide monies for student travel, the completion of graduate degrees, school-based professional development, compensation for substitutes or stipends. (www .fundforteachers.org/apply/guidelines/ny/newyorkcity/individual/03.html)

So if you wanted money for professional development or to pay for subs, you'd be wasting your time applying to this organization rather than immediately looking elsewhere. And if you're unsure whether you're barking up the right tree, don't hesitate to contact the funder in question.

Consider your audience.

Whatever the guidelines state, it's crucial to think about your audience. Who are the people considering your request? First, there are the education officers and staffers at the foundation. And then the organization's board will cast the ultimate votes to give away the cash. So think about it: most of them are probably not educators. They see dozens or perhaps hundreds of applications. And they are always short on time and pressured by deadlines. In some schools, you will also have your proposal vetted by an administrator, so you have to win him over and keep him on your side as well. However, the foundation staff members are likely your most important audience, since they are the ones who sift through all the applications and present arguments to the board about which ones should be funded, so getting them excited about your project is essential. How do you do this?

- Right up front, *provide a short, snappy statement* about what you propose to do and why it's special. Not all guidelines ask for this as a first step, but we think it's really important, especially for the readers who may not have time to read through your whole proposal. This can also help yours stand out from the crowd.

- *Avoid educationese and other jargon.* Those businesspeople on the foundation board probably won't understand it and may resent being made to feel ignorant.

- Along the same lines, *try not to sound formal and academic.* This isn't a graduate research paper. The more you write as an energetic and thoughtful professional able to explain yourself in plain language, the greater the chance that readers will stay with you.

- Remember to *check your spelling and grammar meticulously.* It's surprising how many applications haven't been well proofread. Typos are natural when one is writing. But when errors are left in the final copy, it's easy to interpret this as a lack of commitment, disorganization, or even worse, a lack of the knowledge that a teacher ought to possess. Not the best way to present yourself.

Be concise but thorough.

OK, so if you are going to be complete (but not wordy) in presenting your ideas, what do you need to cover? Most requests for proposals (RFPs, in grant lingo) ask for fairly standard, essential pieces of information, so it's a good idea to address them one way or another, whether the agency specifically mentions them or not:

- What need will your project address?

- What, specifically, will you do to address this need?

- What evidence or research indicates that your approach will be particularly effective?

- What distinguishes your project from others that might be similar? What makes it special and exciting?

- What have you done so far that shows you are on track and ready to make your project a reality? Foundations like a sure bet, as opposed to a vague or undeveloped plan.

- How will you assess the success of your work?

- How will you share your plans and successes with others, to spread the wealth?

- What will it cost (itemized, of course)? (And remember to double-check that you're asking the organization to fund items it typically funds.)

Once you have covered these topics, proofread to cut unnecessary wording. If you can provide the information in fewer words, you'll do the foundation staff a favor and give your ideas more punch. Don't sacrifice important information or ruin your tone, but do look for words that don't contribute to your explanation. This will distinguish you from less articulate proposers.

Pay attention to the proposal or section lengths specified in the guidelines, and stay close to them. Unless your writing is really brilliant, a proposal much longer than the specified limits will make readers impatient—or lead them to reject it out of hand. Conversely, if your proposal is way short of the limit, check to make sure you've really covered everything that needs to be said. You don't want to appear cavalier about your project.

Get constructive feedback.

If you have time before the deadline, let your draft sit in a drawer a few days before revising or proofreading, to develop some perspective on your writing. Feedback from other readers is also extremely valuable; show your work to people who are open to your ideas, but not so close to you that they will hesitate to be honest. Of course, these are all suggestions we'd give to any writer on any topic, whether in a classroom or conferring with a friend over a latte. And just in case you'd like to hear this kind of advice from another source, SchoolGrants (www.schoolgrants.org) offers tips, guidelines, and examples of successful proposals to help teachers with the process.

What are the rewards once you receive a grant? When Janine Givens-Belsley, whom we've quoted in other chapters, worked at a high school for dropouts, she obtained funds from the Chicago Arts Partnership in Education for students to create videos about their individual identities. The kids wrote monologues about themselves and learned how to create storyboards for planning their videos. The funds paid for a graduate student with expertise in videography to handle the technical work. Naturally, the kids loved the project and did some serious writing, planning, and performing, exhibiting a level of engagement and achievement these students and their teacher did not always experience. And the videos were good enough to be displayed in a downtown Chicago gallery. Janine knew, however, that she didn't have the technical ability and wouldn't always have the funds to manage such a complicated project on her own. So she later learned how students could make shorter and simpler videos, by each creating a collection of still pictures about their lives and filming them one at a time while reading their monologues. She now possessed a great teaching strategy to use throughout her career.

In the Classroom

We'll keep this short. We just have a few simple questions: Why do we teachers so often take on all the work ourselves? Why don't we share more of the responsibility with our students? Wouldn't it be cool to have the kids help write a grant proposal? They would certainly learn a lot about the writing process, about developing a good argument, and about the needs of an audience. And their voices might be just the thing to capture the imagination of that foundation officer who has read a million of these proposals and feels as though they are all blurring together into one big plea for cash. Of course you'll need to edit, fill in the gaps, and add your own voice and explanations as well. But think how the kids will react if good news arrives.

This is the approach Greg Michie (1999) took when his students decided, after reading *The House on Mango Street* (Cisneros 1991), that they wanted to invite Sandra Cisneros to their school. This was not a grant, of course, but the idea is the same. As the kids wrote their letters, Greg warned them that she was a busy and popular writer who would probably not be able to respond to such an invitation. But she did, and the kids were overjoyed when she came to visit.

WHAT PRINCIPALS CAN DO

It can take some effort for a principal, nowadays, to pull back from the "tyranny of the urgent," think about the resources beyond the school, and get teachers excited about applying for them. But it's a great motivator when a principal searches for grant opportunities and circulates foundation lists to help pique teachers' interests. Just google "education grants" along with "lists" to find resources. One site we found right away that includes plenty of handy resources, for example, is Fundsnet Online Services (www.fundsnetservices.com). Then learn about teachers' particular passions and energies, and shoot specific information to individuals to encourage them to go after an award.

Once the fire has been lit, teachers who wish to apply for grants may well need some help. Does the central office have a grant writer, or at least an administrator with grant-writing experience, who can lend a hand? Might someone there, or perhaps a board member, have a useful contact with an agency or corporation that funds educational projects to help open a few doors? Is there someone in the community with grant-writing expertise, perhaps at a local nonprofit agency, who is willing to help? Teachers will also need some time to do the background work—reviewing research, pricing materials, or identifying consultants—and to write the proposal. Can they be temporarily relieved of some other responsibility or committee role in order to get the job done? For just like teacher leaders, a good principal needs to see his school in the context of a larger community and actively campaign for its support.

13 Forge Partnerships

How It Helps You

The world beyond our school walls waits with possibilities—businesses, non-profit community organizations, neighborhood groups, universities, experts in various fields. When we connect with them, we widen horizons for ourselves and our students and bring fascinating resources through the schoolhouse door. Conversely, if we neglect them, we reduce the relevancy of school to our students' lives. Steve vividly recalls a chemistry classroom he visited in which students struggled with the definition of a mole (a standard number for counting atoms, in case you've forgotten), its use in calculating amounts of chemicals combining in a reaction, and the amount of the resulting new substance. The kids were trying hard but had no idea that such calculations are used every day by chemical engineers and that high-paying jobs await those who learn how to compute them. Contrast this isolated, in-school activity with the internships developed at Best Practice High School, which led kids like Carlton Jackson to discover a love for videography and Candace Walker to learn the challenges of working at the Rehabilitation Institute of Chicago and then to gain acceptance to Northwestern University (Daniels, Bizar, and Zemelman 2001, 150). Taking the initiative to identify and negotiate a partnership is a major leadership act that brings fresh resources to your classroom and to the school as a whole.

Partnerships not only enrich your teaching and your students' experience of school but also open up new kinds of learning and reconnect you with the energies of the wider world, which is so often shut out of the intense, inwardly focused life of a school. This involvement with the larger social context—with all of its excitement as well as its problems—is one of the hallmarks of real teacher leadership and teacher power. Without it, a teacher is disconnected from the most important forces, issues, and possibilities surrounding her school.

Make It Work

Many cities are home to organizations that promote partnerships between schools and businesses or nonprofit groups. Here are a few examples from around the country:

- Achieve Minneapolis offers a partnership facilitation program (along with other initiatives such as summer job programs and centers for promoting college and careers). More than two hundred businesses and community organizations have participated.

- The Center for Health and Learning in Brattleboro, Vermont, develops school partnerships focused on healthy eating, exercise, and school climate.

- The Lawrence Education Achievement Partners, in Lawrence, Kansas, working with more than ninety business and education partners, promotes partnerships with the Lawrence Public Schools. With the University of Kansas located in the town, many resources are available to create innovative programs to enrich kids' learning.

Let's take a detailed look at one set of partnerships we've followed with great interest. Megan Faurot, as a science teacher at Young Women's Leadership Charter School in Chicago, nurtured a number of outside partnerships to engage her school's students more deeply in her subject. The first, in which she partnered with Friends of the Chicago River, she inherited from a former faculty member. The entire school, seventh through twelfth grades, works on monthlong studies of ecological conditions in the city's less-than-pristine waterway. Students visit the river one grade at a time and gather data under the guidance of an ecology educator from the partner organization. The kids then create projects for an environmental science fair, with Megan distributing the various tasks among the science faculty. One teacher guides the design of the symbol for the project T-shirts. Another arranges for the purchase of needed supplies. A third organizes trip schedules and buses. And so on.

Megan launched a second science partnership after she met and exchanged ideas with oncofertility researcher Theresa Woodruff at Northwestern University. In after-school sessions, twenty-eight of the school's students studied issues of preserving fertility for female cancer patients undergoing chemotherapy.

Then on three Saturdays they worked alongside researchers in Dr. Woodruff's lab. This project was so fascinating to the kids and their families that an information meeting and a follow-up "graduation" ceremony drew 100 percent parent attendance—unheard of at an urban high school.

How did Megan view the challenge of taking time out of her intense schedule to arrange and maintain these partnerships? First, she pointed out, they directly benefited students' learning. Second, they brought additional science expertise to her and her fellow teachers. And with more teaching experience, she found she had more energy for efforts like these. Finally, the partnership work made her feel like more of a professional. "On days when I had meetings at Northwestern, I came to school wearing a suit, and the kids would ask, 'Why are you all dressed up?'" She was modeling a level of social responsibility kids don't always see in their teachers.

University partnerships often take a different form than those with businesses or nonprofits. Frequently, it's the university professor or education department that obtains grant money, approaches a school, negotiates with the principal, and sets up professional development in a particular academic area. Or the university conducts a summer course or training program that teachers can choose to attend. Individual teachers can nevertheless still seek out and establish their own connections, so let Megan Faurot's example inspire you to contact a college or university near you, to see what possibilities lie waiting.

While partnerships provide wonderful connections with real-world experiences that bring learning to life for kids, you'll need to do plenty of careful planning to make them work smoothly and avoid disappointing conflicts or glitches that can arise from unexpected differences in philosophy, style, or agenda. For one thing, the interests and goals of an outside group can be very different from those of the school, and these need to be understood and negotiated from the start. So it is especially important to build relationships and determine common interests. The handbook *Working Collaboratively: From School-Based Teams to School-Community-Higher Education Connections*, from the Center for Mental Health in Schools at UCLA (2008; downloadable at http://smhp.psych.ucla .edu), is very helpful for thinking about this challenge. As one research report puts it (Dunkle and Nash 1989, 35):

In looking at a high risk teenager:

- An educator sees a *student* in danger of dropping out

- A health-care provider sees a *patient* at risk of having a low-birth-weight baby

- A social-service worker sees a *client* who may require public assistance

- A juvenile justice worker sees a potential *runaway*

- An employment specialist sees a *trainee* needing multiple services

- A community or religious leader sees the troubled *offspring* of a personal friend.

The differences can lead to unexpected conflicting decisions and actions by each partner, unless everyone agrees beforehand on the specific goals, action steps, and alternatives that may be needed in case the original design meets with roadblocks.

Megan Faurot encountered just this kind of disconnection when working with her partner organization Friends of the River. The teachers wanted students to collect samples that they would use to complete more extended projects on pollution, while Friends of the River usually approached its expeditions as one-shot occasions to acquaint kids with the various kinds of pollution present and the damage these would wreak. As a result, the teachers found that kids were returning from their field trips without the information they needed. Fortunately, Megan was able to intervene, clarify her requirements, and persuade the organization to alter its usual practices in order to achieve the outcomes she needed.

Working through all the steps to create an effective school-organization collaboration can be a big job—building relationships, formulating an agreement, creating effective working committees, deciding on actions to take, garnering funds, and more. But teachers who decide to spearhead such an effort can make a tremendous contribution to the success of a school. As the author of *Working Collaboratively* asserts, "It is a simple truth that there is no way for schools to play their role in addressing barriers to student learning and enhancing healthy development if a critical mass of stakeholders do not work together towards a shared vision" (Center for Mental Health in Schools at UCLA 2008, 6).

In the Classroom

Since many school-organization partnerships connect directly with classrooms, the application to students is already built into this leadership step. But it's important to think of kids as more than just *recipients* of the effort. Susan Abravanel, in her paper *Building Community Through Service Learning: The Role of the Community Partner* (2003), adds an important piece of the puzzle that not all teachers think about when planning a partnership:

> In service-learning, "youth voice" refers to the inclusion of young people in the planning and implementation of the service opportunity. "When youth voice is missing from a service program, young people may feel more discouraged and alienated. To them, service becomes just one more place in their lives where their ideas are not respected and their contributions are unimportant." (quoted from Education Commission of the States 2001, 1)

> . . . The greater the degree of responsibility given to youth for "planning, decision-making, problem solving and assessing their learning," the better the outcome.

WHAT PRINCIPALS CAN DO

A principal will of course play an essential role in most partnerships. An agreement with a partner organization will very likely require some form of approval from the principal or someone higher up in the school district. The principal may need to act as an advocate if central office administrators need convincing. And many principals themselves take the lead in seeking out partners, though if teacher leadership is to be developed, it's wise to find someone on the faculty who has the interest to pursue the task and then support her on it. The teacher may well need some coaching and opportunities to talk through the various steps and issues, and an experienced principal can help a teacher expand her abilities by proactively scheduling sit-downs for this purpose.

At the same time, it's important not to turn the school into a Christmas tree of programs and partnerships, as often happens in districts where resources are otherwise in short supply. Focus is essential when a school is working to improve. But rather than turn away a teacher who approaches you with a strong passion and a promising contact, look for ways to structure the project so that its activities make use of and emphasize the focus that the school has chosen. Key skills like writing, content-area reading, or problem solving can usually serve a project well and strengthen the kids' learning. Prairie Crossing Charter School, for example, works with a nearby learning farm, where the kids get to plant, tend, and harvest grains and vegetables. At monthly lunches, each grade level takes a turn bringing its crops to be cooked up as part of the midday meal.

But the students also learn about these foods in their science and social studies classes. And they write and perform skits, prepare informational charts and create PowerPoint displays to share their knowledge. The outside partner helps kids see the real-life applications of their classroom learning, and the teachers wouldn't have it any other way.

The Bigger Picture: Distributed Leadership and Whole-School Development

Throughout this book, we've offered ideas for individual teachers who may be working on their own to become active and build power in their professional community. But now let's think about how to develop a whole-school context for this effort.

"What!?" you say. "I'm just one individual teacher. Making the school work as a whole is the principal's job." True. But if your principal is up for creating a stronger teacher community and knows how to set a positive tone, he or she will need plenty of help. And even if the setting is, shall we say, not as upbeat as you might wish, it's still valuable to have a bigger picture in mind to guide you. It will help you understand the dynamics in your school, so you can approach fellow teachers thoughtfully and understand that if some are passive or negative, it's their way of coping with dysfunctional conditions, rather than evidence of a faulty personality.

Programs and mandates for whole-school change have so often been poorly designed or executed over the years that teachers have become understandably hesitant to welcome them. For decades, well-intentioned reforms with good classroom strategies have been launched and then abandoned, often without any real understanding of the culture or social dynamics needed for them to take root in schools. In his study of change efforts in struggling urban schools, *So Much Reform, So Little Change*, Charles Payne observes,

Harried leaders . . . work on this for a little while, then that for a little while, unable to give most problems meaningful attention. . . . Thus, school reform in the 1990's brought forth a remarkable outpouring of activity, but many schools never got past the outward structures of the reforms. . . . New educational programming was constantly being erected over weak social, political, and professional scaffolding. . . . So many efforts continue to proceed in innocence, as if implementation were just a matter of bringing good ideas and clear thinking to the benighted. (2008, 154)

Teachers' resulting skepticism then adds yet another layer of complexity to the setting, so when the next initiative is introduced, it's even harder to get buy-in. Therefore, it's essential to understand the challenges that more active teachers often face and in turn what it takes to make significant change actually happen.

At the same time, we've worked with many schools that *don't* let negative forces take hold and instead build energized, positive, and high-achieving cultures–some of them in the most resource-deprived neighborhoods. We've met wonderful teachers in very dysfunctional schools who not only succeed in their own classrooms but build islands of cooperation and sanity among their colleagues. Of course, if the school's leader does not understand how to create a more effective and collaborative organization, the scope of any effort may be limited. But those who manage to succeed despite difficult conditions are those able to see that embedded in the biggest challenges we face to school change lie the biggest opportunities to create that change.

The Challenges and Opportunities

Altering Teacher Culture in a School

We talked at the start of this book about some teachers' hesitancy to get involved beyond their own classroom. But while individuals choose whether or not to take a role in the teacher community, their one-by-one decisions add up to a larger school culture. In this incremental way, every organization develops norms, usually unspoken and unofficial, that either value cooperation or encourage isolation.

Especially in schools struggling with long-term difficulties, the adults who have tried hard can grow understandably discouraged and may feel threatened by a fellow worker who proposes something different. To the teachers who have worked so hard with so little result, advocacy for change may seem to imply that they haven't done a good job or tried hard enough—and, true or not,

> ## The Big Challenges and Opportunities Inside a School for Achieving Whole-School Change
>
> ▨ altering the teacher culture in a school
>
> ▨ developing a shared vision
>
> ▨ addressing teachers' strong beliefs about teaching and learning
>
> ▨ establishing a process for working on sustained school improvement
>
> ▨ making professional development a process of deep learning and implementation

they resist. And of course these teachers talk to each other every day at lunch and in the teachers' lounge. When resistance becomes pervasive, the inertia affects everyone's actions and decisions.

On the other hand, organizational cultures are not hardened in concrete. We've listened to story after story of a math or a science or social studies teacher, or a twenty-five-year veteran second-grade teacher, who gradually grew to know and trust a colleague, a caring and listening coach or principal, and ended up becoming a devoted user of writing workshop or book discussion circles, or the Responsive Classroom approach. We've found that it's the building of trust among teachers that is the crucial ingredient in actually making a change, and we've described strategies for doing so throughout this book. You can't easily tackle a negative school culture head-on, but building relationships, one at a time, begins to unravel the web that may seem so impenetrable.

Any of us can begin to grow a widening circle of colleagues who talk with and listen to each other, and thus start up a more positive culture within at least part of a school. That's why we so strongly recommend one-on-one conversations and other bridge-building strategies. It's what Janine Givens-Belsley did when she consulted teachers throughout her school to gain scheduled planning time for the faculty (see page 94, in Chapter 9). Janine did not entirely reform the culture of the school, but she did achieve an important improvement in the teachers' work lives. And creating one such success is often a smart way to get started on a larger attitudinal change. Once trust is developed, however, achieving deeper schoolwide change requires further work.

Developing a Shared Vision

Some newer schools that start up as part of a district's reform effort are able to select teachers who enthusiastically support the school's mission and educational philosophy. Others are blessed with a strategically thinking principal or district curriculum director who helps the faculty achieve unity about the nature and direction of their work, maintains a long-range focus on one or two major improvement efforts, and garners resources and time to support them. But many long-standing schools experience no such direction. Teachers have been hired at different times, according to differing educational approaches. Factions have formed over the years, divided in various ways—by generation, race, philosophy, department, or grade level. Priorities change almost yearly. Perhaps a strong-minded principal does mandate a new educational vision by fiat, and it more or less endures, but only until he moves on to another job and a new regime brings in a new set of objectives. As a result, plenty of schools operate simply as a collection of individuals, each operating with no real sense of shared purpose, running on the inertia that long-established organizations acquire. The school vision becomes just a banner or plaque in the front foyer of the building, and few teachers can even tell you what it is.

But think what powerful teaching and learning could be tackled if everyone really did commit to a shared vision. Bringing a disparate group of professionals who have worked for years in a school to the point of sharing a common vision is no easy task, but in their book *Professional Learning Communities at Work*, Richard DuFour and Robert Eaker (1998) make this the cornerstone of their comprehensive approach to school change. Often, it takes some creative, out-of-the-ordinary action to signal that a new effort is truly going to be serious and respectful and thus overcome bureaucracy and skepticism to make change happen, but it is possible.

One very effective strategy was used by Daria Rigney, who served as principal of PS 126, near Chinatown in New York City. Daria began writing frequent letters to the staff, not about particular individuals, but about patterns she observed as she moved about the school—for example, "The read-alouds are great, but are the kids just sitting too long?" Gradually, letter writing grew contagious, and faculty members began to write and reflect. Daria started writing to the kids, as well, on large poster paper that she hung near the front door so the kids could read the letters as they filed in. And, of course, students began writing back, about the life and events of the school.

For the teachers, Daria then introduced lesson studies in which teachers could address problems and design new approaches. When an old-guard group complained that the principal was exerting too much control, she formed a faculty committee to guide professional development—another challenge turned into an opportunity. Teachers were now not only on the same page but taking a major role in guiding the direction of the effort. And no surprise, test scores at the school improved markedly (Zemelman, Daniels, and Hyde 2005, 306–8).

But again, if as a teacher you're not in a position to change the whole school, how might you do this on a smaller scale, within your department or grade-level team or circle of fellow teachers? Karen Sabaka was able to do it with her primary team at Telpochcalli School, even as a new teacher. As we described in the introduction to this book, when she found no coherent direction for literacy instruction, she sought out resources because she needed them herself, and then she convinced her team to learn from them as well. In Karen's school, collaboration is widely encouraged, which made her task easier. In a less supportive atmosphere, you would need to build the relationships with your colleagues first, before making such a proposal, as did Ignacio, Janine, and many of the other teachers described earlier.

Addressing Teachers' Strong Beliefs about Teaching and Learning

Teaching practices are rooted in deep beliefs, derived from teachers' own learning experiences and the culture and social conditions they've dealt with. Sometimes these include experiences or challenges specific to race, gender, class, or community. Likewise, teachers' beliefs may be rooted in what they have *not* themselves experienced. While teachers in professional development sessions are often impatient with talk about underlying philosophies, and prefer concrete strategies they can use tomorrow morning, these beliefs are powerful and important. You may have heard some like these:

- Kids need strong direction!

- No!—kids need more freedom to make choices!

- We've got to focus on the tests!

- No, the tests are worse than useless!

Some of these beliefs are well justified; some may reflect a limited perspective. Either way, changing pedagogy or school structure involves educators revising their beliefs about education itself and their role in it. A one-shot demonstration, a new research study, or even an entire graduate course or workshop series rarely changes such beliefs; often, it just hardens them. Psychological studies show the surprising extent to which people simply hold more firmly to a strong belief in the face of even the most factual challenges (Festinger, Riecken, and Schachter 1956; Baron 1994, 280–89).

No surprise, then, that it looks like trust building over time is probably one of the most important first steps for changing teachers' strongly held beliefs about their work. If a resister feels validated in discussions with a more progressive colleague and believes that person is coming to the table with positive motives and a true respect for her opinions, she is much more likely to listen.

In workshops led by the Illinois Writing Project, which Steve directs, teacher leaders have long made it a point to welcome participants' questions and doubts and hear them sympathetically, rather than avoid challenges or respond defensively. They use writing to enable people to share experiences and ideas that are important to them. And they make sure there's food so that people get to eat together, a powerful symbol of community. These are not incidentals, but essential strategies for opening participants to the possibilities of change. Then something more happens as well. In the workshops, teachers' own writing and sharing sparks new thinking as participants discover their own unrecognized abilities and writing processes. After workshops, when they try out new strategies and observe their own students' enthusiastic responses and increasing skills, their new attitudes grow into actual practice. Still, for a teacher to enact change on his own is difficult and can feel very risky. So the next element that's needed is a structure that creates a larger context of support and commitment in the school.

Establishing a Process for Working on Sustained School Improvement

Without a structured process for pursuing change, good intentions can get lost as all the competing needs in a school assert themselves. We've seen schools where teachers and leaders share the same goals and have strong teaching skills but still struggle to make the changes they agree are necessary. Crises arise. Budgets get cut. New mandates suddenly arrive from above. The planned PD session gets postponed and postponed again. The professional development committee grows disheartened and unsupported. Such struggles in the schools we've worked with tell us that we need a process and a structure for working together and staying on track that is backed by the whole school.

What should such a structure look like? We've found the use of *instructional leadership teams* particularly effective (call them instructional development committees if you like). By focusing on instruction, the team can concentrate on teachers' expertise rather than become bogged down with all aspects of a school's operation. There are a number of steps such a team can take to ensure success:

- *Develop norms and procedures* for working together, dealing constructively with conflicts and disagreements, making decisions, and clarifying power relationships with the principal.

- *Build effective consultation* with all of the school's faculty and staff. A high level of trust is essential so that an instructional leadership team is not perceived as a privileged group, isolated from the rest of the faculty.

- *Employ a cycle of work* that ensures a thoughtful choice of focus as well as an inclusive process for deciding on it and implementing it across the school:
  1. Obtain good, meaningful data to determine a high-priority focus.
  2. Make a decision to adopt that focus through consultation with all the faculty, and then build commitment across the school.
  3. Determine where teachers are and what will best move them to the next step.
  4. Plan the strategies and the resources—time, expertise, readings—to enact that next step, and determine how to organize the effort: By departments? Grade-level teams? Whole faculty? A pilot group with plans to expand later?
  5. Maintain the focus against other intruding challenges, throughout the year.
  6. Develop a culture of shared inquiry and reflection among teachers (in one school, for example, teachers used feedback forms to determine whether they were starting to value observing others' classes and being observed).
  7. Observe how the effort is going.
  8. Plan further steps based on what was achieved and what is still needed.

We began to understand the need for such a structure from our own work with schools. But we also discovered the same kind of work cycle being promoted by the Targeted Leadership Consulting team, who have taught us, in more detail, how to make it work (www.targetedleadership.net).

As a teacher working on your own, you can gather information about such structures, find out which school-reform organizations promote them (there are several), and learn how they work in other schools. You can start conversations about instructional leadership teams or other approaches to distributed leadership in a school. Maybe initiate an exploratory conversation with the principal by showing her an article: "I ran across this piece last weekend on the Web. Do you think it's something we might want to learn more about?"

Or perhaps you are prepared to take a few more risks, as Ignacio Lopez did when he nudged the principal at a high school in Chicago to include classroom teachers on the school's instructional leadership team. The team had been organized as an administrative body, made up mostly of department chairs. When Ignacio proposed adding teachers to the team, the principal hesitated. Ignacio knew their involvement was essential, both to get their input on decisions and to win teacher buy-in to achieve real change in the school. With the guidance of several consultants on instructional leadership teams, Ignacio set up a series of summer meetings for the team, made sure several key teachers were around on the day of the first meeting, and on his own took the step of inviting them to the meeting. When the principal entered and saw them, she at first resisted. Ignacio pleaded and the principal wavered, saying, "OK, just for today." The meeting then focused on planning roles and responsibilities for team members, and after it was over, the minutes were typed up and the classroom teachers' names were on the list. Ignacio also attached a research article on the importance of involving teachers. The principal responded, "OK, we'll try this. But if it doesn't work, the blame will be on you." Fortunately for Ignacio, it *has* worked out beautifully, and the principal is now an enthusiastic supporter of a more inclusive approach.

Making Professional Development a Process of Deep Learning and Implementation

Within a school's improvement process, it's important to think of professional development much more broadly as an effort by which teachers learn as individuals, in groups, and in the whole community, rather than just as information delivery. Traditional PD brings in an expert or an author for a day and then another a few months later. We know of schools that have bought copies of a professional book for all the teachers but never built in time for them to talk about it or plan out how to apply it in their classrooms. The leaders then wondered why nobody read the book or made changes in his teaching. But we also know other schools where coaches have carefully organized teachers' learning and implementation over two or three years, until a well-thought-out and effective new instructional plan has been brought to life.

At Telpochcalli School in Chicago, for example, teachers and the principal together decided that a new structure was needed for their bilingual/dual language instruction. This school in the Little Village neighborhood of Chicago serves an almost totally Mexican American population. Over a period of three years, with the guidance of a bilingual education expert, faculty reviewed curriculum at each grade level, designed a new plan in which social studies and science were taught in Spanish, tried it out and reflected on the results, and designed assessments focused on the specific learning needs and outcomes that the teachers identified.

As an individual teacher, you can try to steer your colleagues, your department, and your principal toward this larger thinking about professional development if they aren't there already. And if you find yourself on a professional development committee or an instructional leadership team, you'll be in a good position to drum up support for deeper PD in your school.

So What Does This All Add Up To?

Educators learn about the social dynamics of classrooms in college courses and in the intense experience of the classroom itself. But we don't usually think about the dynamics of adults in whole schools. Principals (or department heads or other administrative leaders) who possess this kind of knowledge are able to bring a faculty together and harness their various energies to benefit the school and its students. Those who lack this type of skill often try to legislate change through the arbitrary or ineffective exercise of institutional power. They may simply attempt to convey and enforce the mandates coming from the central office. Or they may support one faction in the school, marginalize others, and exacerbate divisions. Whether you work in a supportive atmosphere or under an administration that lacks the skills to develop the school's professional culture, you will need to deepen your own skills in this area.

Like good school leaders, some teachers use effective organizational strategies instinctively; others have absorbed them implicitly, under the tutelage of a skilled mentor. But most of us have just begun to study this process more intentionally. We need to become as proficient as possible in the skills and strategies that can get us from here to there—the trust building, the incremental steps, the carefully thought out strategic actions, the distributed leadership, and the structures and processes that support change. That's what we've explored in this book.

To respond to the challenges of teaching in a complex world and serve children effectively, a school needs as many adults as possible who have developed these skills. While you may not be able to convince everyone in your school to get on board, you can start to develop professionally yourself and promote growth among your close colleagues. In fact, you've already started.

Book Study Suggestions

Learning is frequently a social experience. Though sometimes we feel isolated as teachers, most of us know the benefits of taking time to engage with colleagues. It is in these conversations that we find our own ideas clarified and enriched. While there are many ways to structure a study group, it is most important to foster a climate in which teachers feel free and safe to exchange ideas. Of course, if you are reading this book on your own, the questions can still help you think through the implications for yourself. Here are some guidelines that can help make book study in a group more productive.

Consider Group Size: With a large group, you may want to kick off discussion with a general question and then break into smaller clusters. Often the optimal number is four or five to ensure there is time for all to exchange ideas. The larger group can reassemble at the end to debrief.

Use Study Questions: Some groups find it more comfortable to start with a few questions to get conversation going. There are various ways to use questions.

- Put three or four questions in an envelope and randomly pull them out for discussion.

- Create a chart with two or three starter questions and ask the group to generate more, tapping their own personal interests and needs.

- Decide on three or four questions and divide the group by interest in the various topics. This allows for a more in-depth study.

- Make copies of the suggested questions for everyone and invite discussion without deciding where to start.

Honor the Time Limits: Make sure you have planned a beginning and ending time and *always* honor those times. Teachers are busy, so knowing there will be a time to start and a time to end is important.

Stay Focused on the Topic: Plan a procedure that is helpful without being authoritarian. You might start by deciding on a signal to use when people feel the discussion is drifting and then making a commitment that everyone will help the group to stay focused. Someone other than the facilitator could be appointed to note gently when the conversation begins to get off-topic.

Include Everyone: Keep groups small enough so that even the quietest member is encouraged to speak. Active listening on everyone's part will help. Remember that periods of silence should be expected when people are thinking.

Share Leadership: Rotate group facilitation. Identify several "duties" for the facilitator. Examples might include providing a discussion format, suggesting a big idea from a chapter or group of chapters, and synthesizing or summarizing at the end. Remember that in a study group *everyone* is a learner. This isn't the place for an "expert"!

Create a List of Norms: Simple expectations that are transparent often help study groups function with greater ease and increase potential for success. These can be simple and might include ways to invite a tentative member into the conversation, expectations about listening, time limits if some individual comments begin to go on too long, start and stop times, and a procedure for refocusing.

Set Dates for the Next Meeting: Always leave knowing when you will meet again and who will facilitate.

Engage in Reflection: Stop from time-to-time to reflect on what you are learning and how you might make your group's interactions more productive.

Celebrate Learning: Make sure you take time to enjoy one another and celebrate your learning.

The following questions relate to the content in each chapter. Of course there's plenty more to talk about in each chapter as well. Enjoy!

Introduction: Leadership as Everyday Participation in Your School's Professional Community

1. Give yourself two minutes to describe all of the words or phrases you associate with *teacher power* or *teacher leadership*. Discuss your reactions as a group.

2. Consider the experiences with leadership in schools that you have had. What are some of the models to follow or avoid, as you consider possible roles in the school community for yourself?

3. What are some informal leadership actions that have taken place in your school? Examples could include mentoring a colleague or jointly working on a unit, proposing a new idea in a committee, leading an initiative, and planning an all-school event. Who exercises them? Which ones have been particularly constructive? Have any been negative?

4. What are some of the informal leadership actions that you yourself have taken—perhaps ones that you weren't even fully aware of? How can you and your fellow teachers help each other be more intentional about these?

5. How much influence do you have over the curriculum design outside of your classroom—for example, in a team, grade level, or the school? Would you want more? Why or why not?

6. What do you think of a career and pay ladder that would move you from beginning to master teacher based on criteria other than seniority or graduate coursework? What might be the criteria, and who should decide on them?

7. Informal leadership usually needs the support of the principal, but should not be seen by fellow teachers as merely carrying out the principal's bidding. What steps might a teacher take to balance these needs?

Chapter 1. Start with Yourself

1. The first suggestion in this chapter is to start with your passions. So what are yours, whether in school or outside it (excluding significant others, of course)? How do they compare with others' among your colleagues or in your group? What might you need to do to carve out a little more time for at least one of them? How might they be connected with your school and your classroom in some way (if they aren't already)?

2. What is an area of your profession that you'd like to learn more about? Are there colleagues in your school who share this interest and might want to join you in your exploration?

3. If you have not done so, what would it take to organize a group to walk or exercise together during lunch or after school?

4. How does leadership manifest itself among your students (since it's always there in one form or another)? How might you support this, help it to be positive, and expand it among a wide range of students?

5. Some principals explicitly work to support teachers' leadership development (not the same as identifying pets, however). What steps might you propose, to encourage or help to strengthen this approach?

Chapter 2. Shadow a Student

1. If you haven't yet tried shadowing a student, what do you expect you might see? If you are studying this in a group, compare people's expectations.

2. What do you think you'll need to do to mentally take more of a kid's perspective instead of a teacher's view of what's happening in a classroom?

3. If you (and others) have already tried shadowing, what aspects of the student's experience stood out to you? What are some implications for your teaching?

4. How do you think students could benefit from shadowing other students? What would you hope for them to learn?

5. If your school has a student internship program, what do the students learn from shadowing and working with adults? If it doesn't have this kind of program, do you think one would be useful? How?

Chapter 3. Look Inside the Black Box

1. In what ways, either formal or informal, do you already use research to solve classroom questions and make decisions about what and how you teach?

2. What would you especially appreciate understanding more clearly about your students and their learning? How does your interest relate to that of others in your school or your study group?

3. In many schools, teachers meet in teams or departments to go over student work and discuss their expectations. If you do this with colleagues, what is your experience of the process? If you haven't tried it, what do you think might be the benefits? How might you go about trying to initiate this process?

4. How could you share what you would be learning with other teachers in your school in a way that would gain their interest and consideration? What team-, department-, or school-wide issues could be addressed, using evidence you could collect?

5. What topics would most readily engage your students for in-depth inquiry? How might you learn about their interests? If you haven't tried larger inquiry projects with your students, what concerns would need to be addressed in order to do this?

Chapter 4. Open the Classroom Door

1. To what extent do teachers in your school co-teach or work on planning together? What would entice you or others to do more of this kind of work together?

2. If teachers tend to work in isolation in your school, how might you begin to open things up a bit? With whom might you start? How would you approach him or her? If you are discussing this in a group, what would it take to build trust so you could begin visiting each others' classrooms?

3. If observing other classrooms is regularly practiced in your school, what kinds of benefits have come from it? What challenges have arisen?

4. Reflect on any experiences you've had mentoring and being mentored— whether formally or informally. What do you think are the most important

elements of an effective mentor-mentee relationship? If your school does not have this kind of a program, what steps might be involved in helping to start one?

5. Art Costa's "Cognitive Coaching" is described in this chapter as a constructive approach for observations and mentoring. Have you tried the practice of letting the observed teacher do most of the talking? If so, what does it take to be a good listener? If you haven't tried this yet, what do you think it will take to be one?

Chapter 5. Build Bridges

1. How do teachers at your school get along with each other? Do some feel excluded? Are there divisions of one kind or another? What actions might bridge these divisions? What would make this a worthwhile goal?

2. Think of a time when you saw things very differently from—and perhaps even clashed with—another teacher. Did this relationship (or others like it) ever become less hostile and more productive? If so, how and why did that shift occur? How might you approach such a person in order to have a more positive one-on-one discussion with him or her?

3. Sometimes learning about someone's background experiences completely shifts the way you see that person. Think about any times that has happened to you or to a friend. How did that work for you?

4. Some teachers may initially feel that holding a one-on-one meeting is too "touchy-feely" until they've actually seen a demonstration or tried it. What are some ways you might allay this resistance?

5. How do you handle conflicts between students in your classroom? What are the factors that can make it hard to repair the relationships, rather than just halting the action? What would you like to learn from other teachers about turning conflicts (or at least some of them!) into teachable moments?

Chapter 6. Go Meta

1. What are your own strategies for finding time and focus to reflect on your teaching? How do these compare with approaches used by fellow teachers? What are the advantages, for you, of alone time for reflection versus conversation with colleagues?

2. If you haven't had much time to reflect, what is something you could give up or reduce or postpone (like having a clean house!) in order to find some time?

3. Many people extol journaling, but fewer of us get around to doing it regularly. If you've tried it for your professional work, describe what this was like. How was it useful to you? If you've tried it and stopped, why did you stop and how might you get restarted? If you haven't journaled, give it a try and then reflect on how it went.

4. List the benefits of any of the collaborative reflection activities in this chapter that you've been engaged in or that you'd like to try: for example, planning interdisciplinary projects, discussing books, or holding a "critical friends" discussion. What drawbacks or obstacles might need to be addressed for some of them to work?

5. What conferences, workshops, or presentations outside of school have energized you—or if this has not happened, investigate some promising possibilities (and report them to your group, if you are meeting with one).

6. How might you approach your principal to reserve some time during faculty meetings for broader reflection? Brainstorm some structures that could help insure this time is well used.

Chapter 7. Speak Up

1. What is your particular style and attitude when it comes to speaking up in faculty meetings? Are you someone who naturally speaks up, or is it difficult for you? How do you compare yourself to your fellow teachers on this? What might this suggest you'd need to do to prepare yourself to speak up effectively?

2. Think of a time when you or a fellow teacher brought up a controversial or sensitive topic in a meeting. It may have gone well or badly— but what developments stand out in your memory that you think influenced the outcome? How do these relate to one or more of the steps described in the chapter?

3. Most people find it easier to speak up when working in smaller groups. What would be some factors that would help make expressing ideas in small group discussion safe? What would intimidate people and squelch

conversation? How could you encourage the former, either as a leader of a group or as a participant?

4. This chapter draws heavily on the strategies used by community organizers. Which steps are new to your way of thinking? Which are steps that you have found yourself taking?

Chapter 8. Deal with Committees

1. What experiences, good and/or bad, have you had working on school or district committees? What factors have you found that make the good ones good and/or the bad ones disappointing?

2. For your own development as a professional, what benefits do you see from being on a school-wide committee? What downsides? How do these balance out for you?

3. Some people tend to dominate a meeting and talk a lot, while others sit quietly by. Whether you are a committee chair or a participant, what norms or strategies might help to get the floor shared more equally? How could these be introduced so that people don't feel criticized or singled out?

4. Technology is used more and more in schools. In what ways is technology helpful and/or saving time for committee work in your school? If it is not prevalent where you work, what kinds of help, beyond just word processing, do you picture that it might provide? How could this be further promoted in your building?

5. This chapter stresses the role of the principal in setting up or guiding committees to work well. What would you want to say to your principal about this? (This could range from praise for his or her support to requests of various kinds.)

Chapter 9. Mount a Campaign

1. What broad change efforts have taken place at your school (or others where you've taught). What were teachers' roles in these efforts? What factors appear to have contributed to their success or failure? In what ways did they make your school or your job better or worse?

2. What kinds of time and resources were involved in the changes you considered in question one? What sorts of professional training and/or materials were provided? In what ways were they sufficient or not?

3. What are one or two big needs in your school that you strongly believe should be addressed more fully? How much agreement is there on this, among the faculty or within your study group? If numerous problems are identified, how might you (and the school) thoughtfully choose a first one to work on?

4. Of the various steps in a campaign described in the chapter, which do you think would be especially important to address in your school? Which might be particularly challenging? What, specifically, might be involved in carrying out that step?

5. Assume for a moment that your campaign on the challenge that you've identified is successful. What could be some meaningful kinds of evidence to show the progress and/or concerns as the new effort is carried out? How could the data be gathered in a way that is not too time-consuming or intrusive on teaching and learning?

6. Think of schools or other organizations (businesses, churches, units of government, clubs) that you know of that have made significant changes in how they operate. Big changes might have involved growth, or refocus, re-organization, or perhaps even a relocation. In what ways might they provide models to point the way to meaningful change?

Chapter 10. Talk to the Man

1. What is your own principal like? How approachable? What special interests does he or she have? If this person's style is very different from yours, how do you think you might begin to bridge the gap? How could you show him respect in order to win him to your side without being hypocritical?

2. What about your own attitudes toward authority? How do these affect the way you relate to your principal? In what ways do they help or hinder the relationship?

3. List some issues on which you would like to express your thoughts to the principal. Then list issues your principal might be interested in hearing

about from you. In what ways do these lists overlap? Which ones might be best to start with?

4. What have administrators done that has helped your teaching? If you could be honest with them, what practices would you tell them to expand or change?

5. Communication between a teacher and his or her students mirrors that between teachers and administrators. What are some strategies you use or might think of to help your students learn how to communicate their needs constructively, with each other and/or with you?

6. How do you view your own communication style with your students? Consider with fellow teachers how you might obtain objective feedback on this by studying a book like *The Power of Our Words* and then pairing up to observe each other in the classroom.

Chapter 11. Reach Out to Parents

1. What strategies do you and fellow teachers use to connect with parents? What are some successes that have been achieved by you or other teachers in working with parents?

2. One of the hardest tasks when working with parents is learning to see their kids—and their world— from their point of view. Reflect on times when you may have tried to do this. What stands out to you, now, about the way you responded and started to build trust?

3. What are some strategies outlined in this chapter that you'd like to try? What might be involved in getting them started?

4. If you and/or fellow teachers have had to deal with demanding or critical parents, how did you handle this? What do you think it takes to respond in a constructive rather than a defensive way?

5. A big issue for parent involvement is how much time you should allot for this worthy but time-consuming goal. Reflect on which strategies described in this chapter you presently use or might want to adopt, which are most time-effective— and which ones you could only institute with the active support of your administration.

6. Relationships with parents are influenced not only by individual teachers but also by the whole school. What is the overall practice and tone of this in your school? If you'd like to see it improve, what steps might be helpful?

Chapter 12. Get Grants

1. What are some of the grant opportunities in your area? If you don't have a lot of time to investigate this, how might you divide up the inquiry among some fellow teachers? Or whom do you know beyond your school who might be able to help with this search (reference librarians, for example, who research grant information)?

2. What are some projects that you'd love to try, that would require some extra resources, or some summer planning work, and that might be appealing to an outside donor? How might several teachers in your group or your school collaborate together on such an effort?

3. How might you approach your principal about ideas and help in seeking grants? Consider some of the strategies in Chapter 10 for communicating with principals. How might your request affect how she views your role in the school?

4. Who in your school or your community might help you write a proposal? Think of various people you know—socially, at your church, at the business where a family member works, or at a nearby university.

Chapter 13. Forge Partnerships

1. Who in your community might be interested in getting involved with a special effort at your school? Don't be afraid of making a "cold call" or two to a few influential people in your community. Consider talking with professors at local universities who specialize in your area. If they don't work with schools like yours, ask whether they can point you toward organizations that do partner with schools. And as is true with grants, reference librarians are paid to help you find nonprofits and companies that have partnered with teachers and schools. You never know where you might find some real interest. As you investigate, develop a list of possible partner organizations.

2. What could be a special project that an outside partner would be attracted to? How would it relate to the big improvement goals at your school? How would it connect the interests of the partner with the needs of your students?

3. As you envision a partnership project, what steps might be required to insure that all parties are on the same page with what the project aims to accomplish and how it will be organized?

The Bigger Picture

1. What is the overall attitude at your school toward shared leadership and school improvement? What factors do you think have helped it to be either positive or negative?

2. What are your own attitudes toward shared leadership and school improvement? Think about your hopes, skepticism, or frustrations about these issues.

3. What are some ways that you personally could benefit from improvements at your school? Given the talent pool at your school, what would teachers need to tackle first so that you and they could experience these improvements in your classrooms and work life?

4. Of the various steps outlined in this chapter toward a more collaborative culture and development process, which might need to be worked on at this time at your school? What steps—large or small, with the whole school or with a small group of fellow faculty—could you take to contribute to this effort?

5. Reflect on the strategies that you might use to get your principal to listen to your insights into whole-school change. Since school change often starts with collaborative time for teachers to compare notes and ideas, what are ways that you might persuade the principal to make more of this collaborative time available?

Works Cited

ABRAVANEL, S. 2003. *Building Community Through Service Learning: The Role of the Community Partner*. Denver, CO: National Center for Learning and Citizenship.

ALLEN, J. B. 2007. *Creating Welcoming Schools: A Practical Guide to Home-School Partnerships with Diverse Families*. New York: Teachers College Press.

BARON, J. 1994. *Thinking and Deciding*. 2d ed. Cambridge, MA: Cambridge University Press.

BOUNDLESS READERS' WEBSITE. Retrieved December 12, 2008, from www.rochelleleefund .org/.

BRAIN GYM INTERNATIONAL'S WEBSITE. Retrieved December 11, 2008, from www.braingym .org/.

BRUNICK, N. "One to One Relational Meetings." Unpublished handout.

BRYK, A., AND B. SCHNEIDER. 2002. *Trust in Schools: A Core Resource for Improvement*. New York: Russell Sage Foundation.

CAMERON, J. 2002. *The Artist's Way: A Spiritual Path to Higher Creativity*. New York: Putnam Publishing Group.

CENTER FOR COGNITIVE COACHING'S WEBSITE. Retrieved December 11, 2008, from www .cognitivecoaching.com/.

CENTER FOR THE EDUCATION AND STUDY OF DIVERSE POPULATIONS. Working Together: School-Family-Community Partnerships—a Toolkit for New Mexico School Communities. Retrieved December 12, 2008, from www.ped.state.nm.us/div/rural_ed/toolkit/index .html.

CENTER FOR MENTAL HEALTH IN SCHOOLS AT UCLA. 2008. *Working Collaboratively: From School-Based Teams to School-Community-Higher Education Connections*. Los Angeles: Center for Mental Health in Schools at UCLA.

CHICAGO FOUNDATION FOR EDUCATION. CFE Teacher Grants. Retrieved December 12, 2008, from www.cfegrants.org/.

CISNEROS, S. 1991. *The House on Mango Street*. New York: Vintage Books.

DANIELS, H., M. BIZAR, AND S. ZEMELMAN. 2001. *Rethinking High School: Best Practice in Teaching, Learning, and Leadership*. Portsmouth, NH: Heinemann.

DANIELS, H., S. ZEMELMAN, AND N. STEINEKE. 2007. *Content-Area Writing: Every Teacher's Guide*. Portsmouth, NH: Heinemann.

DARLING-HAMMOND, L. 2005. "Teaching as a Profession: Lessons in Teacher Preparation and Professional Development." *Phi Delta Kappan* 87 (3): 237–40.

DELPIT, L. 1995. *Other People's Children: Cultural Conflict in the Classroom*. New York: New Press.

DENTON, P. 2007. *The Power of Our Words: Teacher Language That Helps Children Learn*. Turner Falls, MA: Northeast Foundation for Children.

DUFOUR, R., AND R. EAKER. 1998. *Professional Learning Communities at Work*. Bloomington, IN: Solution Tree.

DUNKLE, M., AND M. NASH. 1989. "Creating Effective Interagency Collaborative." *Education Week* 8 (25): 35.

EDUCATION COMMISSION OF THE STATES. 2001. *Integrating Youth Voice in Service Learning*. Denver, CO: National Center for Learning and Citizenship.

ELLIS, D., AND K. HUGHES. 2002. *Partnerships by Design: Cultivating Effective and Meaningful School-Family-Community Partnerships*. Portland, OR: Northwest Regional Educational Laboratory.

FACING HISTORY AND OURSELVES' WEBSITE. Retrieved December 11, 2008, from www.facinghistory.org/.

FESTINGER, L., H. W. RIECKEN, AND S. SCHACHTER. 1956. *When Prophecy Fails*. New York: Harper and Row.

FUND FOR TEACHERS' WEBSITE. Retrieved March 21, 2009, from www.fundforteachers.org.

GEVINSON, S., D. HAMMOND, AND P. THOMPSON. 2006. *Increase the Peace: A Program for Ending School Violence*. Portsmouth, NH: Heinemann.

GONZALES, N., L. MOLL, AND C. AMANTI. 2005. *Funds of Knowledge: Theorizing Practices in Households, Communities, and Classrooms*. Mahwah, NJ: Lawrence Erlbaum.

HANKINS, K. 2003. *Teaching Through the Storm: A Journal of Hope*. New York: Teachers College Press.

HARGREAVES, A., AND D. FINK. 2006. *Sustainable Leadership*. San Francisco: Jossey-Bass.

HARWAYNE, S. 1999. *Going Public: Priorities and Practice at the Manhattan New School*. Portsmouth, NH: Heinemann.

HENDERSON, A. T., AND K. L. MAPP. 2002. *A New Wave of Evidence: The Impact of School, Family, and Community Connections on Student Achievement*. Austin, TX: Southwest Educational Development Laboratory.

INGERSOLL, R. 2001. *Teacher Turnover, Teacher Shortages, and the Organization of Schools*. Seattle: Center for the Study of Teaching and Policy.

JACKSON, P. W. 1993. *Life in Classrooms*. 2d ed. New York: Holt, Rinehart and Winston.

LADSON-BILLINGS, G. 1994. *The Dreamkeepers: Successful Teachers of African American Children*. San Francisco: Jossey-Bass.

LAMBERT, L. 1998. *Building Leadership Capacity in Schools*. Alexandria, VA: Association for Supervision and Curriculum Development.

LANTIERI, L., AND J. PATTI. 1996. *Waging Peace in Our Schools*. Boston: Beacon.

LARSON, M. 1997. *Making Conversation: Collaborating with Colleagues for Change*. Portsmouth, NH: Heinemann.

LEITHWOOD, K., AND D. JANTZI. 2000. "The Effect of Different Sources of Leadership on Student Engagement in School." In *Leadership for Change and School Reform*, ed. K. Riley and K. S. Louis, 50–66. New York: Routledge Falmer.

MARKOW, D., AND M. SCHEER. 2003. "The Metropolitan Life Survey of the American Teacher, 2003: An Examination of School Leadership." New York: MetLife. Retrieved from www.metlife.com/WPSAssets/20781259951075837470V1F2003%20Survey .pdf.

MENDEZ-MORSE, S. 1992. *Leadership Characteristics That Facilitate School Change*. Austin, TX: Southwest Educational Development Laboratory.

MICHIE, G. 1999. *Holler if You Hear Me*. New York: Teachers College Press.

MILES, K. H., AND L. DARLING-HAMMOND. 1997. "Rethinking the Reallocation of Teaching Resources: Some Lessons from High-Performing Schools." CPRE Research Report No. RR-38. Philadelphia: Consortium for Policy Research in Education. Retrieved December 11, 2008 from www.upenn.edu/gse/cpre/docs/pubs/rr38.pdf.

MOSES, B., AND C. E. COBB. 2002. *Radical Equations: Civil Rights from Mississippi to the Algebra Project*. Boston: Beacon.

MURPHY, C. 1997. "Finding Time for Faculties to Study Together." *Journal of Staff Development* 18 (3): 29–32.

NATIONAL BOARD FOR PROFESSIONAL TEACHING STANDARDS' WEBSITE. Retrieved December 11, 2008, from www.nbpts.org/.

NATIONAL CENTER FOR EDUCATIONAL STATISTICS (NCES). 2001. *Teacher Preparation and Professional Development: 2000*. NCES 2001–088. Washington, D.C.: NCES.

NATIONAL SCHOOL REFORM FACULTY. 2007–8. *National School Reform Faculty Resource Book*. Bloomington, IN: Harmony Education Center.

NORTHEAST FOUNDATION FOR CHILDREN. Responsive Classroom. Retrieved December 11, 2008, from www.responsiveclassroom.org/.

OAKES, J., AND M. LIPTON. 2006. *Teaching to Change the World*. 3d ed. New York: McGraw- Hill.

PATTERSON, K., J. GRENNY, R. McMILLAN, AND A. SWITZLER. 2002. *Crucial Conversations: Tools for Talking When Stakes Are High*. New York: McGraw Hill.

PAYNE, C. M. 2008. *So Much Reform, So Little Change*. Cambridge, MA: Harvard Education Publishing Group.

SADOVI, C. 2008. "Students Create Biofuel: Algae-Based Fuel Powers VW Van to Sears Tower and Back." *Chicago Tribune*. May 30, p. 17.

SALACUSE, J. W. 2005. *Leading Leaders: How to Manage Smart, Talented, Rich, and Powerful People*. New York: AMACOM.

SAMFORD UNIVERSITY. CENTER FOR TEACHING, LEARNING AND SCHOLARSHIP. Retrieved December 11, 2008, from www.samford.edu/ctls/.

SEBRING, P. B., E. ALLENSWORTH, A. S. BRYK, J. Q. EASTON, AND S. LUPPESCU. 2006. *The Essential Supports for School Improvement: Research Report*. Chicago: Consortium on Chicago School Research.

Silins, H., and B. Mulford. 2002. "Leadership and School Results." In *Second International Handbook of Educational Leadership and Administration*, ed. K. A. Leithwood and P. Hallinger, 561–612. New York: Springer.

Smith, M., and J. Wilhelm. 2002. *Reading Don't Fix No Chevys: Literacy in the Lives of Young Men*. Portsmouth, NH: Heinemann.

Stevens, W. D. 2006. *Professional Communities and Instructional Improvement Practices: A Study of Small High Schools in Chicago*. Chicago: Consortium on Chicago School Research.

———. 2008. *If Small Is Not Enough . . . ? The Characteristics of Successful Small High Schools in Chicago*. Chicago: Consortium on Chicago School Research.

Stigler, J., and J. Hiebert. 1999. *The Teaching Gap: Best Ideas from the World's Teachers for Improving Education in the Classroom*. New York: Free Press.

Targeted Leadership Consulting's website. Retrieved December 11, 2008, from www.targetedleadership.net/.

Tatum, B. 2003. *Why Are All the Black Kids Sitting Together in the Cafeteria?* New York: Basic Books.

University of Texas at Austin. WINGS Online. Retrieved December 11, 2008, from https://uteach.utexas.edu/go/wings/Mentor-Development/.

Vopat, J. 1998. *More than Bake Sales: The Resource Guide for Family Involvement in Education*. Portland, ME: Stenhouse.

Zemelman, S., H. Daniels, and A. Hyde. 2005. *Best Practice: Today's Standards for Teaching and Learning in America's Schools*. Portsmouth, NH: Heinemann.

Zemelman, S., P. Bearden, Y. Simmons, and P. Leki. 2000. *History Comes Home: Family Stories Across the Curriculum*. Portland, ME: Stenhouse.